JURISMANIA

Jurismania

THE MADNESS OF
AMERICAN LAW

Paul F. Campos

New York   Oxford
Oxford University Press
1998

Oxford University Press

Oxford   New York
Athens   Auckland   Bangkok   Bogotá   Bombay   Buenos Aires
Calcutta   Cape Town   Dar es Salaam   Delhi   Florence   Hong Kong
Istanbul   Karachi   Kuala Lumpur   Madras   Madrid   Melbourne
Mexico City   Nairobi   Paris   Singapore   Taipei   Tokyo   Toronto   Warsaw

and associated companies in
Berlin   Ibadan

Published by Oxford University Press, Inc.
198 Madison Avenue, New York, New York 10016

Oxford is a registered trademark of Oxford University Press

Library of Congress Cataloging-in-Publication Data

Campos, Paul F.
Jurismania : The madness of American law /
by Paul F. Campos
p. cm   ISBN 0-19-510785-3
1. Law—United States—Methodology.   2 Judicial process—
United States.   3. Culture and law.   I. Title.
KF379.C36   1998
349.73'01—dc21   97–17940

Printing (last digit): 9 8 7 6 5 4 3 2 1

Printed in the United States of America
on acid-free paper

Contents

For Kaylah and Leia

It is from my experience that I affirm human ignorance, which is, in my opinion, the most certain fact in the school of the world.

MONTAIGNE

Preface

"I always wanted you to admire my fasting," said the
hunger artist. "We do admire it," said the overseer, affa-
bly. "But you shouldn't admire it," said the hunger artist.
"Well then we don't admire it," said the overseer, "but
why shouldn't we admire it?" "Because I can't help it,"
replied the hunger artist. "I couldn't find food I liked. If I
had, believe me, I should have made no fuss and stuffed
myself like you or anyone else."

FRANZ KAFKA, "A Hunger Artist"

In his book *Eat Fat* Richard Klein points to "a growing awareness
that the whole [American] culture of dieting and rigid exercise is the
root cause of the fat explosion." Klein believes that "the diet system
produces the disease that the system is charged with curing. Fat is
decreed to be poison, but the antidote, diet and exercise, makes
more fat. . . . There is reason to think that if doctors stopped threatening people about their weight they would be thinner."

Klein's account of why Americans are fat taps into the deep psychology of obsessive behavior. His is a sort of "anti-diet" book,
based on the insight that it is in the nature of obsessions to cause us
to pursue something in such an excessive way that we not only fail in
our quest, but end up producing the opposite of whatever it was we
were pursuing in the first place.

This book is, in part, about how the obsessive pursuit of law in
contemporary American culture tends to produce a kind of bureaucratized anarchy. It is intended for the general reader whose experience of American law has made him or her wonder if there might

not be something fundamentally wrong with a system of social coordination and dispute processing that "works" in the ways ours does. (Notice, by the way, how apologists for American law always claim in its defense that "the system works" without ever bothering to explain what they might mean by this.)

Why is American law so complex, so hypertrophied, so obsessively perfectionist, and (therefore) so terribly expensive? Why is our legal system so eager to bring every variety of social interaction within its ever-expanding gaze? And why do Americans of every social background and political orientation persist in believing that what they think of as "the law" can succeed where politics and culture fail?

I believe the answers to these questions are interrelated and have much to do with the excessively rationalistic structure of modern life. *Jurismania* tries to show how the pathological features of American law are themselves symptoms of an often irrational worship of rationality that characterizes much of our public culture. Indeed, what I call "jurismania" is at bottom a mania for giving reasons—a kind of widespread cultural syndrome that is the product of a neurotic goal. That goal is to rationally resolve social disputes that are not amenable to rational solution, but that those suffering from the syndrome have been acculturated to believe both must and can be resolved through the use of reason.*

Although our legal system is perhaps its favorite locale, the general syndrome manifests itself wherever the forms of cognitive dissonance that mark modern moral discourse are particularly acute. Thus the book eventually branches out from the specific analysis of American law to touch on the broader underlying crisis in contemporary moral and political life. In one sense this book is a diagnosis

---

*Throughout this book I will speak of "reason" without giving an account as to what precisely this word is supposed to signify. This isn't an oversight. In an important sense many of the extreme claims rationalist ideology makes for what it calls "reason" are enabled by the ever-shifting meanings it assigns to this rather mysterious term. Indeed, as we shall see, "reason" is to the rationalist what "God" is to the theologian: that entity which by definition always is whatever it must be in order to do the metaphysical work attributed to it.

not merely of a sick legal system, but a sick culture: a culture whose metaphysical axioms, if they were taken seriously, would require people to believe that choosing between the morality of Socrates and that of Hitler is no different from choosing between Coke and Pepsi. As it happens, almost all human beings are incapable of believing such a thing; and I try to show how, as a consequence, the political and moral rhetoric of our public culture is plagued both by severe conceptual incoherence and by that dogmatic denial of any such incoherence a rationalist culture always elicits from its defenders.

Until fairly recently the central thesis of this book—that, in its more extreme manifestations, what Americans call "the rule of law" can come to resemble a form of mental illness—would have seemed an exercise in frivolous or irresponsible hyperbole. Perhaps it still does. But can anyone who followed the O. J. Simpson affair dismiss such an idea out of hand? It is too easy to discount such events as representing anomalous departures from a healthy norm. Consider the sordid national spectacle which is the Paula Jones–Bill Clinton litigation. Or observe the effects of a decision to initiate yet another of our intermittent ceremonies of special prosecutorial zeal. By now we are all familiar with the routine: small armies of lawyers will demand documents, subpoena witnesses, convey hearings, cite laws, interpret regulations, unearth precedents, impanel grand juries, bring indictments, and, in the course of their diligent investigations, almost incidentally destroy the political effectiveness of our most important public figures. To what end, exactly? To uphold "the rule of law"?

Legal academics, dedicated as we almost always are to the defense of that law, are not inclined to ask such questions. Still, as America prepares to indulge in yet another of its periodic spasms of legalistic sanctimony, can we who have helped bring about such spectacles of political self-immolation state with real confidence that the benefits are worth the costs of what we claim, over and over again, is "the best legal system in the world"? How many times must we partake in a species of symbolic human sacrifice, performed by our relentlessly bureaucratic priesthood, before we begin to question this culture's obsession with the pursuit of what it calls the rule of law? And when will we begin to consider that it is precisely our addiction to law that produces so much of the very lawlessness our law condemns?

Jurismania isn't an argument for irrationalism, nihilism, anarchism, or any other -ism. It no more endorses messianic visions of a libertarian social order than it does unlimited regulatory zeal. (For those who care about such things, its author's politics are essentially those expressed by Ernest Hemingway's very short story, "Old Man at the Bridge.") The book doesn't deny that, in their proper place, law or reason or legal reason are good things; it doesn't even deny that the present excesses of American law might be a form of *necessary* madness. But it tries to describe those excesses for what they are, without rationalizing them away or otherwise minimizing the social damage they cause, and without proposing the sorts of facile "solutions" to which the legal-minded are so prone. This book asks us to recognize the vice of legal gluttony, and to learn to admire the virtue of a kind of jurisprudential fasting. That, indeed, is its solution.

Paul F. Campos
Boulder, Colorado
July, 1997

Acknowledgments

Jose Luis Campos, Sarah Krakoff, Robert Nagel, Michael Perry, Steve Smith, and Christine Trend read the entire manuscript of this book, and made many helpful suggestions. So did Peter Berkowitz and Richard Posner, who commented on drafts of individual chapters. Members of the law faculties at the University of Michigan and Southern Methodist University heard talks based on what became chapters of the book; I am grateful for their engaged comments, and hope the manuscript retains some evidence of those interchanges. The editorial suggestions made by several persons at Oxford University Press were models of tact and discretion. Tavia Fielder Colving provided me with valuable research assistance, as did the scholarly research funds of the University of Colorado School of Law.

All books are more or less collective efforts; this one is especially so. The work and thought of my colleagues Rebecca French, Bob Nagel, Pierre Schlag, and Steve Smith has played an indispensable role in the gestation of this book. *Jurismania* is in many senses a reflection of their collective influence. In particular, justice demands I thank Steve Smith for bailing me out of many a jam—intellectual and otherwise—in which I found myself during the course of the book's composition.

Finally, I thank Kaylah Campos Zelig and Leia Campos Zelig for making this book possible.

1

AMERICAN CULTURE
AND THE MADNESS OF LAW

> As formerly we suffered from crimes, so now we suffer
> from laws.
>
> TACITUS

In the middle of a dull April afternoon I answer a telephone call
from a reporter with the *New York Times*. The reporter wants to talk
about Mahmoud Abdul-Rauf's constitutional rights. He informs me
that Abdul-Rauf, a shooting guard for Denver's professional basketball team, has just been suspended without pay by the National
Basketball Association. Apparently, he is refusing to stand at respectful attention during that playing of the national anthem that
always takes place before the beginning of any significant American
sporting event. It turns out there is actually a league rule that requires all players to stand at respectful attention during the playing
of the *Star-Spangled Banner.* Abdul-Rauf is claiming that he considers standing for the national anthem a violation of his religious
obligations and furthermore considers the U.S. flag and anthem
"symbols of oppression." On what I hope is a slow news day, this
rather absurd little dispute has been seized on by elements of the
national media. "What about the First Amendment?" the *Times*
reporter asks. Here we go again, I think: the law talk is starting.

In contemporary America there seems to be no issue of public life
that can spend more than a few minutes on the national radar screen
before legal modes of argument begin to take over. All types of
social disagreements seem to be routed almost inexorably into the
tendentious jargon and intellectually impoverished categories of

legal reasoning, until everyone from Alan Dershowitz to the guy fixing your radiator insists on giving you his opinion about fundamental rights, or presumptions of innocence, or probable cause, or —God help us—"what the Constitution requires."

If it should so happen that you are someone who is intimately familiar with these forms of argument and, as a consequence of that familiarity, don't much believe in them any more, all this law talk is going to get on your nerves. In the case of the Abdul-Rauf "controversy" my irritation is exacerbated by the fact that I do have some questions I'd like to discuss with the *Times* reporter, questions in which he seems to have no interest. For example, what does it tell us that the NBA actually has a formal rule addressing this particular contingency? How is it that Abdul-Rauf claims to believe his Islamic faith prohibits him from saluting the flag when no sect of Islam enforces such a prohibition? And is he ever going to get his game back together?

But the reporter doesn't want to hear about any of that. He wants to talk about the First Amendment.

Games Without Frontiers

Abdul-Rauf's refusal to stand for the national anthem violated the NBA's code of conduct for its players, which explicitly requires all players to stand at respectful attention during the playing of the *Star-Spangled Banner*. In the jargon of the law, this provision created a contractual obligation that Abdul-Rauf was required to fulfill unless the obligation itself was superseded by some other legal rule or norm. How, we might wonder, did the code of conduct come to address such a seemingly arcane contingency? Yet the specific answer to that question is in all likelihood not as important or interesting as the mere fact of the provision itself.

The NBA's provision is a prime example of an ongoing process we might think of as the juridical saturation of reality. In the modern world, law is everywhere. And although, as the taciturn epigram at the beginning of this chapter testifies, this process is hardly unique to modernity, the increasingly bureaucratic structure of modern life has allowed that process to accelerate to a truly striking extent. In particular, anyone who compares the legal domains of our society to those of the premodern state immediately becomes aware of a tremendous and ever-increasing contraction of formally unregulated social space. Consider the old Russian folk saying, "Russia is large and the Czar is far away," or that quaint expression from the Anglo-American past, "going to law." These proverbial phrases captured the reality of a state and its law that was elsewhere: an elsewhere both remote from everyday existence and hence more than a little exotic. Not so long ago the notion of "going to law" was for most Americans much like the idea of going to Romania; while to the Russian peasant the Czar was akin to the Holy Spirit—an awesome symbolic force that nevertheless seemed largely absent from the ordinary workings of day-to-day life.

Today all that is changed, changed utterly. Now law comes to us, whether we want it to or not. Legal modes of vocabulary and behavior pervade even the most quotidian social interactions; the workplace, the school, and even the home mimic the language of the law, and as a consequence replicate its conceptual schemes. Indeed we may be seeing the fulfillment of Max Weber's grim prediction that in the postindustrial world everything will eventually be subjected to formal rules, if only because the gradual elimination of unregulated human conduct is necessary to the efficient functioning of both the modern bureaucratic state and advanced consumer capitalism. In such a juridified future we will all, no doubt, be "free"—free, that is, to perform our exquisitely regulated labor, in order to fulfill those cultural imperatives that even now impel us to acquire an ever-expanding list of luxurious necessities.

What is clear is that all of us move through a social space that becomes more saturated with rules: regulations that attempt to control the minutiae of our social roles in ever-more obsessive detail. Not so long ago informal social pressures would have been exerted on a basketball player to stand for the national anthem; if those failed, perhaps an equally informal exception to the general cultural norm would have accommodated his peculiar beliefs. Or perhaps not. Today such examples of the power of civic etiquette are becoming rapidly beside the point. Today, the player is told that he has "consented" to the requirement that he stand, which after all has been made "explicit" somewhere(!) among the multifarious clauses of his "freely negotiated contract."

The motto of contemporary American life might well be an ironic variation on the drug culture's slogan, "Legalize it!" We strive to legalize every actual or potential human conflict so that all aspects of our existence can benefit from the advantages of the rule of law. And really, who could object to that? The subtext of the NBA's anthemic rule is the unspoken message of American legal ideology: make every obligation, every right and its corresponding duty, sufficiently explicit so that none may have cause to complain that they were not given proper notice, that they were denied due process, or that they are being obliged to do or not to do anything other than what the various legal and social contracts they have chosen to enter into explicitly contemplate. It all sounds reasonable enough, save for one problem: taken to the extremes manifested in the following modest excerpt from the National Collegiate Athletic Association's vast regulatory code—styled, revealingly, as its "Constitution"—this idea becomes nothing less than a form of cultural madness. (Painful as this brief selection is to read, grappling with it is a necessary exercise for the lay reader who needs to experience, if only for a moment, the occupational angst of the ordinary lawyer, who must plow through muddy fields of similar documents every day.)

Constitution, Article 1
1.3.1 Basic Purpose.
The competitive athletics programs of member institutions are designed to be a vital part of the educational system. A basic purpose of this Association is to maintain intercollegiate athletics as an integral part of the educational program and the athletes as an integral part of the student body and, by so doing, retain a clear line of demarcation between intercollegiate athletics and professional sports. . . .

Article 2
Principles for Conduct of Intercollegiate Athletics
2.01 General Principle

Legislation enacted by the Association governing the conduct of inter-collegiate athletics shall be designed to advance one or more basic principles, including the following, to which the members are committed. In some instances, a delicate balance of these principles is necessary to help achieve the objectives of the Association.

2.2 The Principle of Student–Athlete Welfare

Intercollegiate athletics programs shall be conducted in a manner designed to protect and enhance the physical and educational welfare of student–athletes.

2.2.1 Overall Educational Experience

It is the responsibility of each member institution to establish and maintain an environment in which a student–athlete's activities are conducted as an integral part of the student–athlete's educational experience.

Article 13

13.1 Contacts and Evaluations

Recruiting contacts (per 13.02.3) and, in Divisions I and II, telephone calls with a prospect (or the prospect's relatives or legal guardians) by institutional staff members and/or representatives of the institution's athletics interests are subject to the provisions set forth in this bylaw. . . .

13.1.2.3 General Exceptions

. . . (f) **Unavoidable Incidental Contact.** An unavoidable incidental contact made with a prospect by representatives of the institution's athletic interests [shall not be subject to this regulation], provided the contact is not prearranged by the representative or an athletics department staff member, does not take place on the grounds of the prospect's educational institution or at the sites of organized competition and practice involving the prospect or the prospect's team (i.e., high school, preparatory school, two-year college or all-star team), is not made for the purpose of recruitment of the prospect, and involves only normal civility. . . .

13.4 Recruiting Materials

(c) **Newspaper Clippings—Division II Only.** Newspaper clippings may be sent to a prospect, but may not be assembled in any form of scrapbook. . . .

13.7.5 Entertainment/Tickets on Official Visit

13.7.5.1 General Restrictions.

An institution may provide entertainment, which may not be excessive, on the official visit only for a prospect and the prospect's parents [or legal guardian(s)] or spouse and only within a 30-mile radius of the institution's main campus. . . .

13.7.5.5 Student Host.

The institution may provide the following to a student host entertaining a prospect:

(a) A maximum of $20 for each day of the visit to cover all actual cost of entertaining the prospect (and the prospect's parents, legal guardian, or spouse), excluding the cost of meals and admission to campus athletic events. These funds may not be used for the purchase of souvenirs such as T-shirts or other institutional mementos. . . .

13.7.5.8 Normal Retail Cost.

If a boat, snowmobile, recreational vehicle or similar recreational equipment (including those provided by an institutional staff member or a representative of the institution's athletic interests) is used to entertain a prospect or the prospect's parents or legal guardians, the normal retail cost of the use of such equipment shall be assessed against the $20-per-day entertainment limit; further if such normal retail cost exceeds the $20-per-day entertainment allowance, such entertainment may not be provided.

The NCAA's efforts to regulate the conduct of its revenue-producing sports is a rather frightening example of both juridical saturation and of what might be called the Will to Process. This latter phenomenon is a product of the assumption that substantive flaws in the nature of a practice can be neutralized or even eliminated by crushing those flaws under a sufficiently vast mountain of administrative rules and procedures. Hence the NCAA produces a 300-page code, with its thousands of sections, subsections, and subsections of subsections, in an attempt to anticipate and resolve everything from the most mundane conflicts of interest to the most exotic administrative contingencies.

Yet despite—or perhaps because of—this appearance of regulatory comprehensiveness, the NCAA code actually fails to address the central problem of college athletics. The most notable substantive flaw in the practice of big-time intercollegiate sports is this: the NCAA regulatory code's self-proclaimed basic purpose of ensuring that the athletes whose performances fill huge stadiums and guarantee billion-dollar television contracts are nevertheless otherwise ordinary college students is blatantly at odds with limitations imposed by what might be called "reality." It is, after all, exactly as realistic to expect great running backs to be adequate scholars as it is to expect great scholars to be adequate running backs. Everyone knows that, to the extent major college football and men's basketball hold themselves out as mere extracurricular activities in the life of otherwise ordinary college students, the two sports are and must be fundamentally fraudulent practices.

I don't want to sound too sanctimonious about this—I love college football as much as anybody. Anyone who grew up in Ann Arbor, Michigan, or Columbus, Ohio, in the 1970s will understand when I admit that the Michigan–Ohio State games of my youth remain some of the most intense emotional experiences of my life. The essential hypocrisy of big-time college athletics doesn't rank high on America's list of social crises, nor should it. But that hypocrisy can't be eliminated, or even significantly reduced, as long as a fundamental contradiction remains between the actual and the professed goals of the revenue-producing college sports. And that fundamental contradiction will stay in place so long as certain college sports are driven to produce millions of dollars of revenue. Such sports must be professional in all but name.

The NCAA's response to this inescapable and corrupting dilemma is straightforward: legalize it. The governing body of college athletics is gradually extruding a regulatory text that reads like some crazed amalgam of the *Tractatus Logico-Philosophicus* and the *Uniform Commercial Code*. We might note that this particular code is addressed to a social context in which, to choose from an almost endless list of examples, college basketball coaches earn millions of dollars pimping for athletic shoe companies by requiring their players to wear those companies' shoes while at the same time making pious noises about the "integrity" of their sport (translation: the players must work for free), and in which it was revealed recently that one out of every seven football players at a prominent university has been arrested at least once during his tenure there as a "scholar–athlete," leading the country's best-known sports magazine to call for the school to eliminate its football program. Meanwhile, as high school basketball prodigies hold lavish press conferences at which they announce *in advance of their matriculation* that they will grace some ivied campus for but a single year before departing to an unambiguously professional team, subsection 13.7.5.5 of the NCAA code is trying to regulate the purchase of T-shirts.

These phenomena may seem paradoxical, but in the context of American culture they are actually part of a standard operating procedure. A sphere of human activity that is understood to be corrupt in some essential way—college sports, political fundraising, the cigarette trade, and so on—is therefore subjected to the most exquisite regulatory schemes, as if saturating the activity with juridical requirements will somehow transform its rotten essence into something rich and strange.

Again, painful as they are to read, the NCAA regulations are symptomatic and thus worth grappling with. Indeed, even the minuscule selections I have quoted illustrate several professional deformations that mark the pathologies of the American legal mind at its most florid. For instance, one would think the "General Principles" found in Article 2 could only be taken seriously by persons who believe that platitudes have special and perhaps even magical powers whenever they are cast into sufficiently legalistic language. Of what possible use can it be to inform institutions of higher learning that "athletics programs shall be conducted in a manner designed to protect and enhance the physical and educational welfare of student–athletes?" And who has ever doubted that anything like a sufficiently broad list of abstract principles delimiting any complex set of considerations could avoid being "balanced" against each other? These banal utterances might be understood as part of an incantation that attempts to dissolve through verbal magic the ineliminable conflict between the financial structure of major college sports and the educational role of the university. Would not a person who truly believed in the efficacy of such provisions be laboring under some sort of delusion? Yet as we will see, lawyers are in one sense professionally obliged to believe that legal language has such powers.

Or consider the definition of an incidental contact, not subject to the multitude of restrictions on other sorts of contacts between college recruiters and their quarry. This definition exempts such a contact as long as, among many other things, it was "unavoidable," not prearranged by the recruiter, and "not made for the recruitment of the prospect." From a pragmatic perspective the entire subsection would more sensibly read "incidental contacts are exempt." (After all, truly incidental contacts are by definition neither avoidable nor prearranged, and the restrictions on where incidental contacts can take place merely illustrate how certain contacts are not truly incidental.) Here again we see the lawyer's characteristic urge to give words efficacious powers through acts of compulsive elaboration and repetition.

Or we can puzzle over the almost Kafkaesque flavor of the regulation allowing newspaper clippings to be sent to a prospect, but not "in any form of scrapbook." Such obsessive attention to what are surely meaningless distinctions is a product of a hypertrophied rationalism: of a rationalist ideology that can envision no limitations to its power. As a consequence of their insistent need to exercise control, out-of-control regulatory schemes end up producing rules more absurd than any that could be generated within a more modest cognitive framework. Increasingly, the legal institutions of our culture seek to regulate social interaction at the most maniacally fine level of detail, until the bureaucratic schemes of law's empire begin to have more than a passing resemblance to Kafka's nightmare world of inexplicable orders handed down through the agency of some anonymous, unappeasable force.

In this regard, consider the interaction between articles 13.7.5.1, 13.7.5.5, and 13.7.5.8. The first article states that entertainment "which may not be excessive" can be provided for a prospect, and "the prospect's parents or legal guardians, or spouse." The general word "excessive" is then rendered superfluous by a $20-per-day entertainment limit; that limit is further elaborated on by a provision that specifically addresses the rental of recreational vehicles (why is this necessary?); and this further subsection adds both an obviously redundant rule forbidding more than $20 to be spent on such things, and a potentially confusing omission that implies to the lawyerly mind either that (1) this rule doesn't apply to the entertainment of prospects' spouses because spouses, unlike parents and guardians, are not mentioned in this particular subsection, or (2) spouses may therefore not ride on rented snowmobiles at all. The quest for regulatory comprehensiveness thus produces a surreal mishmash of redundant and contradictory rules.

From a certain perspective all this appears, as I say, to be a manifestation of a kind of madness. Reading through the NCAA code, the proverbial visitor from another land might conclude a lawyer is a person who believes that certain words have magical properties, that there is no such thing as an excessively fine analytic distinction, and that regulatory schemes can be both comprehensive and self-executing. And the visitor would be correct—*to a certain extent*. Yet ironically most lawyers are better protected against the madness of law than the American public itself, bombarded as that public is by cultural imperatives demanding that it take law's own representations of what law is and does with the utmost seriousness. By contrast, what (usually) keeps the madness of law from becoming the madness of lawyers is a necessary—and indeed a therapeutic—inauthenticity. This, too, must be part of the properly socialized lawyer's persona.

Let us return to Mahmoud Abdul-Rauf's constitutional saga. What was it that led Abdul-Rauf to claim his religious beliefs prohibited him from "conforming his conduct," as lawyers say, to the standards enunciated in the National Basketball Association's regulatory manual? Here we must enter briefly into the technical arcana of employment law. To wit: if Abdul-Rauf was merely undertaking a *political* protest by refusing to stand for the anthem, as his comments about "symbols of oppression" implied, he would under current legal doctrines have no ground for complaint if he were penalized for failing to adhere to the terms of the standard player contract. On the other hand if his refusal to stand was a consequence of a sincerely held *religious* belief, then his employer could be required to make "reasonable accommodations" for the practice of that belief. Given this, it is easy enough to imagine the practical outcome of a conversation between Abdul-Rauf and his agent, or some other lawyer, in which he was apprised of these particular facts.

Every lawyer knows with some part of his or her brain that "sincerely held belief" is often a term of art meaning something like "invented on the spot for the purposes of litigation." And yet every lawyer and law professor quoted in the newspapers the day after the Abdul-Rauf story broke treated the player's profession of a previously unknown dictum of Islamic law as if this professed belief were simply a peculiar aspect of the player's worldview. Were these lawyers being disingenuous? It depends on how you define that term. The legal academics among them may well have been so naive, so disconnected from the actual practice of law, that the most plausible account of why Abdul-Rauf claimed a religious ground for his actions may not have occurred to them at all. But the practicing lawyers must surely have known what the most likely explanation was for Abdul-Rauf's statements.* Yet to "know" is a complex concept—especially for a lawyer.

Lawyers make claims not because they believe them to be true, but because they believe them to be legally efficacious. If they happen to be true, then all the better; but the lawyer who is concerned primarily with the truth value of the statements he makes on behalf of clients is soon going to find himself unable to fulfill his professional obligation to zealously represent those clients. Another way of putting this is to say that inauthenticity is essential to authentic legal thought. Practicing lawyers must often maintain a peculiar mental state in which they fail—authentically—to recognize the inauthenticity of their claims. A lawyer must be authentically inauthentic, so much so that he or she can honestly(?) echo Samuel Goldwyn's observation that the most important quality in successful acting is sincerity. "Once you've learned to fake that," Goldwyn observed, "you've got it made." It is to say the least an awkward state of mind, but it is the essence of the legal form of thought. And it is this form of thought that, ironically, preserves the lawyer's sanity in the face of the madness of law.

---

*In fact, one day after saying that he would rather retire than make any concession to the NBA rule, Abdul-Rauf agreed to stand respectfully during the national anthem, with his hands covering his face in a traditional posture of Islamic prayer. The one-game suspension cost him approximately $31,000 in lost salary, and would have cost him an additional $31,000 for every game he would have missed while adhering to the dictates of his "sincerely held religious belief."

A lawyer learns the art of indulging in the most extreme forms of law talk, with all their apparent reliance on verbal magic, with all their obsessional and delusional qualities, while never fully internalizing many of the beliefs this talk seems to require. Indeed, a good lawyer keeps his or her grip on reality by remembering, on appropriate occasions, that law is ultimately just a way of talking. For in the end, law can't be treated as an accurate reflection of the social world it is attempting to regulate without doing serious damage to the intellectual and emotional capacities of people who treat it as if it were. Imagine trying to understand college sports through the lens of the NCAA regulatory code. That would be akin to studying American culture by going to Disney World for a week and then flying back to the Sorbornne (not that this method hasn't been employed by certain audacious savants), or attempting to discern a presidential candidate's actual beliefs by reading his party's convention platform. It would be like trying to improve your social life by studying the representations of successful social interaction found in beer commercials—and then drinking lots and lots of beer.

Celluloid Heroes

In the midst of the 1996 presidential campaign, Senator Robert Dole was criticized for condemning the moral messages conveyed by various Hollywood films he had never actually seen. The response of Dole's staff to this criticism was truly remarkable. The staff arranged a "media event" at which Dole would view a suitably uplifting movie (*Independence Day*) and then praise the film for upholding values he claimed the films he criticized had slighted or ignored. The particularly brazen aspect of this campaign stunt was that his staff had written the speech containing Dole's purported reaction to *Independence Day* before he had seen the film! When reporting on these events, the journalist Michael Lewis pointed out that most members of the national press have become so inured to this sort of thing they no longer even notice the multiple levels of fraudulence it involves. Lewis commented that in his view, "The only way to stay sane is to assume the American people don't pay any attention to this kind of crap."

That, in a nutshell, is how lawyers stay sane when they are forced to profess allegiance to, and even in a peculiarly limited sense believe in, the sorts of things proclaimed by texts such as the NCAA's regulatory constitution. Unfortunately, it is often part of their job to make sure the rest of us don't have that particular option.

2

THE COLOR OF MONEY

In their majestic equality our laws forbid the rich and
poor alike to sleep under bridges, to beg in the streets,
and to steal their bread.

ANATOLE FRANCE

In Gilbert and Sullivan's *H.M.S. Pinafore*, the Boatswain praises
Ralph the able Seaman with the following song:

He is an Englishman!
For he himself has said it,
And it's greatly to his credit,
That he is an Englishman!
For he might have been a Roosian,
A French, or Turk, or Proosian,
Or perhaps Italian!
But in spite of all temptations
To belong to other nations,
He remains an Englishman!

This is supposed to strike the audience as absurd: Ralph can hardly
be praised for resisting the temptation to be what he cannot be in
order to remain what he surely is—an Englishman. Today, when we
have come to accept that so much of reality is socially constructed
rather than being a reflection of some objectively immutable order
of things, there is no longer anything absurd about the idea of
choosing to remain a member of one nationality rather than becoming something (or someone) else. Indeed, it seems that various
markers of personal identity are becoming ever-more transitory and

permeable; and thus in contemporary American culture it is now widely accepted that persons can alter not just their nationality, but their class status, their religion, their sexual orientation, and even their gender.

Interestingly, one social marker seems relatively immune to this protean flux: race. For example, in our public culture O. J. Simpson's "blackness" is understood to be just as much a brute fact about him as the fact that he has two arms and two legs. In America at the end of the twentieth century the idea that Simpson can choose to remain black remains as ridiculous as the idea Ralph could choose to remain English seemed to his fellow countrymen 120 years ago.

A very different perspective on the nature of racial identity comes to us from the former heavyweight boxing champion, Larry Holmes. In response to a white reporter's questions about growing up black in the working-class town of Easton, Pennsylvania, Holmes asked the reporter if she had ever been black. Startled, the reporter admitted that she had not. "Being black," Holmes said, "is hard. I used to be black—when I was poor."

This cryptic statement concerning the complex relationship between the concepts of race and class in American society might serve as an epigram for the first O. J. Simpson trial. Indeed, Holmes's observation reminds us of how O. J. Simpson was in a unique position to exploit that relationship. For Simpson is certainly "black" in the Holmesian sense that his public racial identity made possible the sorts of arguments his defense was able to exploit so well—arguments about the racist proclivities of the likes of Mark Fuhrman. But Simpson is also "white"—again in Holmes's sense—in that he could actually afford to pay for such an elaborate exploitation of those arguments. By successfully synthesizing these aspects of Simpson's identity his defense was able to produce what even in victim-obsessed America remains a true cultural rarity: the oppressed millionaire.

But such observations merely remind us of how all the hand-wringing over race in the Simpson affair has only helped obscure the more salient question of social class. Can there be much doubt that if Simpson had been poor or working class, then, black or white, the overwhelming circumstantial case against him would have led his public defender to convince him of the wisdom of pleading guilty to a charge of second-degree murder? That if, in the unlikely event there had been a trial, it would have taken more than perhaps two weeks? Or that the outcome of such a trial would never really have been in question? These are not, of course, original observations. All throughout the trial we heard again and again from a host of legal commentators how only the circumstance of Simpson's wealth made it possible for him to take full advantage of the many generous features the American legal system makes available to those criminal defendants who can afford to employ them. This, we were led to understand, was a shame. So in a sense the class angle was not ignored during the Simpson trial. Yet these very same commentators seemed to believe it was simply a regrettable (and immutable) feature of social life that only rich defendants have the resources to exploit the exceedingly complex structure of contemporary American criminal jurisprudence.

Now what I find most interesting about this attitude is its orientation toward the very problem it identified. Imagine if Simpson were to receive the sort of defense that could have been put up by an earnest public defender. Then, after the inevitable conviction, the American public is informed that unfortunately only white people are allowed the sort of defense that might have spared the former football star. Needless to say such a claim would be utterly unacceptable. Yet when faced with the disturbing fact that, despite the egalitarian rhetoric of our legal system, only rich people can afford much of what is referred to as "the rule of law," the reaction of the legal establishment is akin to the fatalistic resignation of a Dostoyevskian peasant confronting the onset of another Russian winter. "You shouldn't blame us for this state of affairs," explain various apologists for the legal status quo. "That's just the price we pay for having the rule of law. Justice, after all, isn't cheap." This is generally followed by utopian statements to the effect that the government "should" make "high quality" (a.k.a. expensive) legal services available to everyone: statements that to be actualized would necessitate the sort of wealth redistribution that would in turn require the elite legal establishment to surrender some of its economic and social privilege, which of course it isn't going to do.

Am I being unfair? Sure—but not *that* unfair. Let us imagine a certain figure: we'll call him a typical liberal legal academic, or ATLLA for short. ATLLA believes in what he thinks of as the rule of law. Now we must understand that this thing he believes in, and which he dedicates much of his professional life to defending and reproducing, isn't anything nearly as capacious as what it sounds like. After all, in its literal sense the phrase "the rule of law" would also signify how they do things in other countries—countries whose legal systems ATLLA admittedly doesn't know much about. For ATLLA, the rule of law is in all likelihood really the rule of *Harvard* law, which is to say of the legal process jurisprudence handed down to a generation of legal academics during their student days in Cambridge, Massachusetts, or some very similar sort of place. I once produced a catechismic imitation of the legal process style that tried to capture both the ideological commitments underlying its methods and the consequences for thought and prose that tend to follow from faithful attempts to carry out the style's rigorous jurisprudential requirements. Here is a representative sample:

What judicial procedures do these methods involve?

They involve, firstly, a careful not to say exhaustive review of all the relevant legal materials whose meaning, properly interpreted, might throw light on the proper resolution of the sorts of cases and controversies that courts display a special institutional competence toward resolving; secondly, the formulation of various complex interlocking directives by means of which the properly interpreted meaning of those materials may be made synonymous with those interpretations that flow from the proper deployment of those interpretive methods which give the meaning of those materials a public and formal character, thereby making that meaning accessible to everyone who has undergone a socialization process resembling that to which students at elite American law schools were subjected, circa 1958; thirdly, the acceptance of the pragmatic yet principled dictum that law is a purposive activity which continually strives to solve the basic problems of social living; fourthly, the full recognition of the indispensable role played by that most lawyerly virtue, procedure, in assuring a kind of objectivity to what would otherwise degenerate into an unconstrained act of judicial fiat; fifthly, the establishment of the principle or public norm that decisions which are duly arrived at as a result of duly established procedures for making decisions of this kind ought to be accepted as binding on the whole society unless and until they are duly changed; and sixthly, the sobering realization that the only alternative to regularized and peaceable methods of decision is a disintegrating resort to violence.

This is a parody, but not a very gross one. Indeed, several phrases in the passage were lifted whole from the locus classicus of the movement, Harvard law professors Henry Hart and Albert Sacks's eternally unfinished treatise, *The Legal Process* (tentative draft, 1958). Legal process pedagogy, and even more so the vision of law from which the teaching method springs, requires an exhaustive engagement with the materials and procedures of the American legal system that in certain circumstances can begin to resemble a type of repetition compulsion. (To be clear: it isn't that careful review of legal questions is a bad thing. But then neither is washing your hands—unless you feel compelled to do it forty-seven times per day.) The emphasis on "getting it right," and the agonized struggle to define just what that might entail, produce a distinctive vision of law that is totalizing, relentless, and mostly oblivious to such crass considerations as time, money, and possible limits to the powers of human reason. Nevertheless, as a matter of what can best be understood as a highly contingent quirk of social and intellectual history, the formal characteristics of this jurisprudence have combined with the political orientation of the Warren and Burger Supreme Courts to produce what ATLLA now thinks of as not so much a particular vision of law, but rather as nothing less than "the" rule of law itself.

It has not been noted that one of the most fascinating aspects of the Simpson trial was how it provided Americans with an unusual opportunity to see an almost pure example of this rule of law in action. After all, given the economic consequences of taking what is called the rule of law seriously, it isn't surprising that fully 95 percent of all criminal convictions in this country are obtained without a trial, and that an even higher percentage of civil litigation is settled without the benefit of a courtroom verdict. Those trials that do take place are themselves almost always much more cursory than what rule of law ideology would consider consonant with an adequate exploration of the relevant legal materials. But Americans are by reputation practical people; and most of the time we find it is simply too expensive to enjoy the full benefits of the rule of Harvard law. Indeed, in a sense the American legal system doesn't collapse only because of a tacit understanding that its formal rules must never be followed. Most legal actors perceive, if only unconsciously, that any serious effort to actually instantiate the rule of law would produce results similar to one of those work actions where a labor union brings a factory almost to a halt by the simple expedient of requiring its members to follow the work rules supposedly in force. Nothing would destroy our legal system more effectively than a sincere attempt to enforce its laws.

The Simpson trial was different. Because of the political importance of the case to the Los Angeles District Attorney's Office, and because of the almost unprecedented social position of the defendant (with the doubtful exception of Aaron Burr, Simpson was the most celebrated American ever to be charged with murder), there was essentially no economic barrier to transforming the rule of law from classroom theory into courtroom practice. Here was a truly singular occasion where considerations of scarcity would not rein in the enthusiasm of the participants. This circumstance allowed platoons of lawyers and "experts" deployed by both the prosecution and the defense to exploit the full panoply of options made available to them by the structure of our criminal justice system. Dozens of witnesses were questioned and cross-examined for days at a stretch; evidentiary rulings, interpleadings, and motions of every conceivable sort took up hundreds of hours; indeed, the impaneling of the jury and the intermittent expulsion of nearly half of its original members alone took up far more time than was spent on, for example, the debate and ratification of the original U.S. Constitution.

None of this, of course, seemed to make much of an impression on the surviving jurors, who disposed of the issue at hand with a brisk indifference to the evidence that itself suggested the futility of the whole absurd exercise, and which indeed brought to mind the relative advantages of trial by ordeal. In the months since that surreal climax it has often been said that recommendations for reform should not be based on the Simpson trial, given that it was in so many ways a unique event. Such statements are of course accurate as far as they go, but consider what they overlook. For again, what was most unique about the Simpson trial was precisely that it provided an example, *in the practice of an actual courtroom rather than in the theory of the law school classroom,* of modern American rule of law ideology in full bloom. Here, in the scarcity-free space of Judge Ito's court, we saw the consequences of actually taking the rule of Harvard law seriously. Here we saw in their most extreme form various characteristic features of the American legal system that are usually muted by the constraints of fiscal and psychological reality. These include (but are not limited to) the worship of procedure; the attempt to rationalize every aspect of the decision-making process; the distrust of spontaneous action; the demand for something approaching perfection in the handling of the relevant legal materials; the urge to maintain a continuous and pervasive managerial control over every participant; and, above all, the daunting complexity of the rules that such a system requires. It is of course hyperbole, but is there also not some truth in the claim that this, after all, is how the American legal system is *supposed* to work? Indeed, we might want to think of the Simpson trial as a year-long demonstration of the ways in which much of what is called the rule of law resembles, in its most florid manifestations, a culturally sanctioned form of obsessive-compulsive behavior.

Perhaps the question on which the professional defenders of the legal status quo need to focus their attention is this: just whose interests are served by this social structure and the behavior it elicits? Who benefits from the immense and even neurotic complexity of the modern American legal system? We already know the answer to this question—indeed, our friend ATLLA knows the answer. That is why he "supports" increased funding for legal aid; that is, in part, why he will from time to time undertake to represent a death row inmate for free. *Pro bono publico,* "for the public good." That is a noble-sounding phrase, but let me suggest a scheme that might benefit the wretched refuse of our teeming shores in a more meaningful way. Of course it isn't going to happen; almost nothing recommended by well-intentioned academics ever happens. Still, imagine a system of criminal trials in which juries were seated by picking the first twelve people in the pool who did not know the defendant or the victim. Imagine a system in which witnesses could say what they had to say in their own words, without constant interruptions for evidentiary rulings by control-obsessed advocates and decision makers. Imagine a system where these advocates played a relatively minor, facilitating role in the proceedings. Imagine a system in which, because of such features, it was simply expected as a matter of course that a well-conducted, fully adequate trial would take a day or two, with the occasional proceeding lasting as long as a week. Finally, picture a system of criminal justice where mixed panels of legal professionals and lay judges would engage in a pragmatic, mostly nontechnical dialogue in the course of deciding the fate of the defendant. Now despite their exotic flavor these suggestions are not mere pipe dreams. In fact something like this is what the criminal justice systems of many other developed nations already resemble.

What social consequences would flow from such a scheme? Note that in this sort of system a middle-class person would be able to afford a defense to a serious criminal charge that would in most respects be comparable to what a rich person could procure. Furthermore a system along these lines would give the poor criminal defendant a realistic chance of having his or her true legal expenses defrayed by the government, or absorbed by a lawyer who under such circumstances would not need to make a huge economic sacrifice to adequately represent an impoverished defendant.

By contrast, in the American legal system elaborate procedures designed to ensure fairness often end up ensuring something else altogether. Consider the following example. In high-profile criminal trials—those that tend to feature rich defendants or, as in the Oklahoma City bombing case, defense lawyers who for whatever reason are willing to exhaustively litigate a trial at government expense—the process of interrogating prospective jurors now sometimes takes several weeks. The naive justification for allowing such an extensive process is that it weeds out prejudiced persons from the jury pool. The sophisticated justification is that the strenuous efforts of both prosecution and defense to stack the jury with persons prejudiced in their respective favors will cancel each other out, resulting in a jury that manifests a rough balance of various prejudices. Now note how this same result could be achieved at least as effectively (and at much less expense) by simply employing the English system of selecting jurors at random. But of course such a system deprives wealthy defendants of the advantages to be gotten from the hiring of high-priced jury selection consultants, who tend to defeat comparatively overworked and understaffed prosecutors in the playing of this particular psychological and demographic game.

Such examples remind us of how the Will to Process—the urge to rationalize, codify, administrate, proceduralize, and otherwise complicate a system of social coordination and dispute processing—increasingly makes that system available only to the social elites who have the resources to manipulate it. They also remind us that academic visions of what law is have political consequences, although rarely in the way law professors imagine. What matters about what legal academics teach their students is not the substance but the form; or rather in this case the form *is* the substance of what students learn. For instance, while ATLLA believes he is demonstrating in his criminal law classroom that the death penalty is unconstitutional, what he is really demonstrating is how to produce a system that will not only execute a poor man, but will also spend $2,000,000 trying to determine whether that man was represented adequately by a court-appointed drunkard who was paid $500 for his services. Justice, we are told, isn't cheap. Indeed it isn't: especially when, despite the egalitarian rhetoric within which they are routinely cloaked, the excesses of American legal ideology tend to transform the rule of law into a kind of luxury good.

We may be sure the defenders of what they call the rule of law will find themselves horrified by any suggestion that our legal system should grant its subjects fewer rights and options; that it should be less rationalist and more open to the role of chance in human decision making; or that it should give up on any ambitions to achieve a celestial degree of what we call "justice."* But how can such a system ensure the undeniable benefits of what lawyers refer to as "procedural due process"? How will it weed out the effects of prejudicial evidence and prosecutorial misconduct? How, in a word, will it be fair? Yet the question the defenders of the status quo need to face—that we need to face—is "fair" in comparison *to what*? In comparison to a system that has, partially through the efforts of ATLLA and his legion of academic fellow travelers, become so elaborate, so complicated, so unwieldy, and therefore so expensive that as a practical matter it exists almost exclusively for the benefit of the upper class?

"The rich," noted F. Scott Fitzgerald, "are different from you and me." "Yes," replied Ernest Hemingway, "they have money." In America today, what is celebrated in legal academic circles as the rule of law often functions as a complex cultural mechanism for the protection of class privilege. This statement isn't merely a rephrasing of the banal platitude that the rich will always be able to afford more "justice," so-called, than the poor. For what the Simpson criminal trial illustrated with special clarity is that the answer to the specific question of *how much more* justice the rich can afford is always a function of the particular characteristics of a specific legal system. The grand irony of the American legal system is to be found in precisely this: that it is by their very efforts to make law "fair"— efforts that perversely make the benefits of law ever more dependent on the expertise of a specialized sector of the upper class—that lawyers in this same sector of the upper class have made many of the benefits of law all but unavailable to anyone other than members of the class to which those lawyers belong.

Yet the blindness so many contemporary American legal thinkers display toward how legal ideology plays an important role in the creation and maintenance of the class structure from which those same lawyers benefit is hardly a new or unique phenomenon. Indeed, one might even remark that in their majestic equality *our*

---

*"I fear those big words that make us so unhappy." James Joyce, *Ulysses*.

laws grant the poor as well as the rich the "right" to, among many other things, the full analytic rigor of procedural due process, the endless elaboration of evidentiary questions, the exhaustive deployment of the appellate courts, and the most socially irresponsible representation money can buy.

3

THE ANARCHIC PANOPTICON

> What have our legislators gained by selecting a hundred
> thousand particular cases and actions, and applying a
> hundred thousand laws to them? This number still bears
> no proportion to the infinite diversity of human action
> ... the most desirable laws are those that are rarest, sim-
> plest, and most general; and I even think it would be bet-
> ter to have none at all than to have them in such num-
> bers as we have.
>
> MONTAIGNE, "Of Experience"

In the heart of Boulder, Colorado, nestled against the very spot
where the high plains disappear abruptly into the foothills of the
Rocky Mountains, Alfalfa's Market represents the cultural epicenter of what the natives refer to, without apparent irony, as "our
healthy Boulder lifestyle." Here one can purchase dairy-free cheese
and wheat grass lemonade; here the glistening breasts of free range
chickens—birds we can only hope chose poulterer-assisted suicide
—offer themselves up to those of us who still eat animals. (Twin
bumper stickers spotted on a Volvo in Alfalfa's parking lot: "Pro-
child, Pro-choice" and "Friends Don't Let Friends Eat Meat." I
wonder for a disorienting moment if the car's owner sanctions the
eating of unborn herbivores.)

Wander the richly laden aisles of Alfalfa's and you will encounter
beautiful, recently divorced women of a certain age, their voices full
of money, their faces already beginning to suffer from the wrinkled,
emaciated look that eventually marks everyone who worships at the
shrine of the ubiquitous and unappeasable god "Health." Here, too,

you will find Boulder's college students, well-heeled hippies accompanied by their babushka-clad dogs, buying the $30 per pound smoked salmon they will carry back to the communal condominium in new Range Rovers and Saabs. Their bumper sticker of choice: "Live Simply So Others May Simply Live."

Shopping at Alfalfa's is an ethically and intellectually challenging task. It seems every other item advertises itself as organically grown, or pesticide free, or gathered under humane conditions (humane for whom is not specified). The heretofore simple act of buying eggs has come to require the interpretation of a rigorous moral code that regulates jealously what before were considered fairly unproblematic acts. It is all very much like the Book of Leviticus, except here the wrath of the God of Israel has been replaced by snide looks from Birkenstock-clad trust fund babies who otherwise spend their unlimited leisure time worrying about cholesterol levels, the Dalai Lama, and the price of IBM.

Boulder, it would appear, is being transformed into a little Nirvana for a certain discrete sector of the American upper class. The town is fast becoming a kind of fantasy camp for aging yuppies: stereotypical limousine liberals with bottomless reservoirs of empathy for everyone who can't afford to live within an hour's drive of these blessed environs. Open space laws both ensure that the price of housing stays astronomical and the population remains more or less all white; ferocious anti-smoking ordinances are enforced with unrelenting zeal; and the local constabulary makes sure the panhandling Deadheads on the mall don't interfere with one's legal right to buy a $1,500 Navajo blanket, or anything else a person might need to climb the north face of K2, or at least look like he might.

Alfalfa's Market functions as the spiritual center of that informal but vigorous hedonistic cult, Our Healthy Boulder Lifestyle. Its credo is disarmingly simple: if you eat only what's good for you, exercise with monk-like devotion, and avoid unreasonable risks, you will never die. On pleasant days—which means almost every day; that, too, is part of OHBL—initiates of the cult stroll the downtown pedestrian mall, searching for the perfect latte, "marked" with a hint of foam. Watching these ideal specimens of Nordic health and good looks I notice everyone seems to be a sort of light golden color, like extras from a Leni Riefenstahl epic.

In Boulder the *übermensch* has been transformed into a socially conscientious shopper. It's 3:30 on a Wednesday, and I'm reminded of Michael Moore's comment at the beginning of his documentary film, *Roger and Me*. The son of an autoworker, he surveys various denizens of the San Francisco cafe set whiling away the languorous hours of another weekday afternoon and asks himself, *Doesn't anybody here have a job?* No, actually.

Emblazoned above the main entrance of Alfalfa's is the Alfalfa risk-free guarantee: *"Your Alfalfa's shopping experience is risk-free and 100% guaranteed."* We are further assured that although "many of our choices may be new and unfamiliar to you," we are permitted to experiment to our hearts' content. If any element of our experimentation goes wrong—if, for example, we find ourselves revolted by dairy-free cheese—we can return our purchase and receive a "no hassle" refund. "So take your shopping cart and your taste buds on a new adventure—risk free."

Here we encounter the apotheosis of the regulatory state, and indeed the whole point of striving to achieve total juridical saturation: the final elimination of risk itself. The good citizens of Boulder may spend all day dangling from the sheer rock face of a local canyon, or they may enliven the evening by ingesting hallucinogenic mushrooms before driving back up that canyon without remembering to turn on their headlights, but if they should be so unfortunate as to purchase a bruised apricot, they retain, if they made that choice at Alfalfa's, an unimpeachable legal right to return it for a full refund. There's a rule, you see, that says they can. Oh, if only all of life could be like shopping at Alfalfa's! Why isn't life itself risk free and 100 percent guaranteed? And indeed if you live in some place as aggressively utopian as Boulder, where everyone owns a turbocharged Saab equipped with a ski rack and two enormous dogs, you may actually expect an answer to this question.

Asserting the inalienable right to the pursuit of some version of hedonistic immortality is one common reaction to the sheer pointlessness of so much of modern life. The urge to regulate—to medicalize, juridify and police every act of labor or play—is in part a contemporary by-product of the need to deal with the loss of any broadly held belief regarding what the point of human existence might entail. The idea seems to be that, if we no longer have any sense of why we should choose to live in this or that fashion, let us at least make these meaningless "lifestyle choices" as properly informed consumers.

The cryptic message of American consumer culture could thus be decoded as, "Feeling existential dread? Buy something!" A particularly extreme manifestation of this tendency is the magazine *Consumer Reports*, with its unconscious and apparently arbitrary ideological commitment to putting the supposed rights of consumers always and everywhere before the interests of producers, whomever they might be. This, we are to assume, is the American Way. Read *Consumer Reports* and you will be told which flavor of chocolate ice cream tastes best, along with a helpful description of what chocolate ice cream is "supposed" to taste like. Never will you, the fully informed consumer, choose the extravagant creaminess of Häagen-Dazs when—for seventeen cents less!—you could have experienced the socially conscious goodness of Messers. Ben & Jerry, who do good by tasting good. In quests such as these do we squander hours, days, and years.

The ultimate dream of our contemporary regulators is to harness technology so that every choice, no matter how trivial, can be imagined to be the choice of the fully cognizant and freely choosing liberal individual self. Go ahead and buy that pint of Häagen-Dazs Chocolate Chocolate-Chip: one day soon, after you have struggled to open the new safety-sealed lid, a holographic image—a veritable regulatory homunculus—will spring forth to lecture you on what, precisely, this gastronomic indulgence is doing to your arteries, and what you could have done with the seventeen cents *Consumer Reports* wants to help you save. And remember: it will all be done so that *you* can freely make the choice that the hedonistic puritans who regulate our lives have already determined to be the *right* choice, the "healthy" choice of conscientious citizens everywhere.

"Cigarettes are bad for you," notes Richard Klein, "that is why they are so good." The charm of the sublime, life-wrecking narcotic that is tobacco remains wholly opaque to Boulder's local Committee for Public Safety, who have made it almost impossible to have a legal smoke anywhere within the town. Even bars have been transformed into "atmospherically healthful environments," which when you think about it makes little more sense than requiring brothels to be havens of chastity. A few months ago a small scandal erupted when a local production of the play *Grand Hotel* was threatened with municipal sanctions for allowing an actor on-stage two or three puffs of a cigarette, for the sake of the drama's *mise-en-scène*. The theater's owner reacted by threatening to—what else?—sue the city, for violating the First Amendment no less.

I myself, having been in this regard emasculated by the voices of my so-called education, find it impossible to smoke. I thus pretty much limit my attempts to engage in what used to be known in the police states of the Eastern Bloc as "anti-social behavior" to occasionally concocting one large, very cold martini—what in a more civilized era E. B. White referred to as "the elixir of quietude." (Instructions: the night before your symposium, put shaker, glasses, and Bombay gin in the freezer. Mix four parts gin to one part Noilly Pratt, over ice that is cold enough to give off wisps of smoky vapor when it makes contact with the air. Serve with a twist of lemon.) This mixture is guaranteed to transport the soul into regions of contemplative clarity, regions that remain utterly inaccessible to worshipers of the bitch goddess Health. Speaking of which, I have broken—definitively—with my previous flame, Winona. And why? Simply because Uma, bestower of blessings, smokes three packs of Marlboros per day, lending her voice a raffish, Bacallesque charm no straight man can resist.

Welcome to the Working Week

Reader, if your day is at all like mine your alarm goes off at something like 6:17 A.M. As you stumble toward its digital glow it is worth reflecting on the fact that until very recently there *was* no such thing as "6:17 A.M." For almost all of human history, people got up around dawn, or toward the middle of the morning, or were late risers. The sort of regulatory exactitude made possible by the concept "6:17" is yet another of the dubious advances that technological progress has bestowed upon the contemporary world. Because of such advances in human consciousness you know you have exactly forty-three minutes before you must depart your domicile for the place of your employment. Within that time you will perform the series of complex ablutions required of a well-socialized individual of your station in life, and you will don that delicately calibrated semiotic system—your clothes—that represent to its other members your precise position within an invisible but complex hierarchy. You will then head for the freedom of the open road.

Driving to work, you pass an automatic speed monitoring device that announces you are moving at precisely twelve miles per hour above the posted limit. As you slow to seven miles above the limit (the exact speed at which you calculate no officer will ever stop you) you are nearly run off the road by a truck that features a toll-free number under the legend "How Am I Driving? (We Hire Only Safe and Courteous Drivers)." You remember with a pang of mingled guilt and annoyance that the deadline for the car's annual required emissions test has passed; you then circle in a parking lot for nine minutes because the only available spaces are three of the eight new ones your employer is now legally required to reserve for handicapped individuals, but that in fact are usually occupied by the vehicles of various able-bodied persons who have the temerity to declare themselves "disabled."

Once at your desk you find that your supervisor expects you to spend all day generating memoranda designed to document the many derelictions of a co-worker who, because he can no longer be fired without what the legal system will recognize as "just cause"— and really, who but a misanthrope could object to such a transparently fair requirement?—clings to his sinecure with all the tenacity of a python. He, like most other members of the small class of persons who the firm ever actually fires, will eventually sue the company for wrongful discharge, despite the hundreds of hours that have been spent on mind-numbingly bureaucratic tasks designed to gather evidence indicating why it was imperative their employment be "terminated."

This particular task is especially aggravating to you because by the end of the week you must draft a memorandum for the firm's lawyers, describing in rich detail all the risks involved in the firm's development of a new product. The purpose of this memorandum is to allow the lawyers to produce the legally required prospectus that will announce a new stock offering by the firm's parent company. The legal system's justification for this requirement is that the prospectus will give investors the information they need to make a rational investment decision. The firm's lawyers, however, have already told you to make the risks associated with the issuance of the stock sound much more severe than they actually are because, as they explain it, the institutionalized habit of risk-averse lawyers of putting grim-sounding warnings in prospectus literature has made investors almost completely indifferent to such warnings. Because this kind of lawyerly boilerplate is so commonplace it no longer has any real informational value and is therefore ignored. And precisely because it is ignored, the lawyers explain, there is no real disincentive to producing unduly pessimistic warnings that can later be cited, if necessary, for the proposition that investors were "fully informed" of the risks involved in their investment decision.

You then find yourself spending twenty minutes of your lunch hour arguing with some poor telephonic drone, who is technically the representative of the insurance company that is supposed to provide your family's medical benefits. This conversation, which will be replicated several thousand times this day all across America, is a product of the following game-theoretical dilemma. Insured persons realize that because they pay for covered medical care in advance, they have every incentive to exploit the inevitable ambiguities and loopholes that arise in the extremely complex rule systems of modern insurance regimes, thereby making sure the insurance covers as many medical costs as possible. Insurance companies are, of course, aware of these same incentives; hence they often follow an informal policy of simply refusing, as an initial matter, to pay for any medical costs whatsoever. The two groups then engage in strategic posturing via the agency of the telephonic drones, each citing an inexhaustible supply of rules, policies, procedures, administrative regulations, and so on, and intermittently threatening each other with formal legal action.

By the day's end you will join millions of similarly situated persons emerging from towers of glass that, at precisely 5:07 every afternoon, disgorge rivers of their exquisitely regulated occupants. You are "free," now, to head for your home and family: venues that are themselves becoming more and more permeable to various rapidly proliferating networks of bureaucratic imperatives. Indeed, although your spouse asked you to pick up a pint of Häagen-Dazs on your way home, even now a voice from the car's radio is intoning that the Center for the Elimination of Socially Irresponsible Pleasure has determined a pint of gourmet ice cream contains more fat than twenty-two strips of bacon, so on further reflection perhaps you should buy some 97 percent fat-free SnackWell Bars, 100 percent guaranteed to mimic the flavor of real chocolate. . . .

This is our modern panopticon. This is a world so saturated with juridical and quasi-juridical imperatives that there is almost no social interaction not subject to possible surveillance and regulation via the agencies of the state. All of us might as well be walking around with toll-free numbers on our backs, under the legend "How Am I Living? (We Socialize Only Docile and Compliant Citizens)." Despite our culture's continuous celebration of human freedom, and despite the libertarian rhetoric of "choice" that pervades the propaganda to which the citizen-consumer is continually exposed, you and I, dear reader, possess considerably less freedom than we might imagine. Indeed, there are days when the juridical saturation of our lives ensures we have fewer real choices than a free-range chicken. We are all fast becoming slaves, as it were, of modernity and its ubiquitous rules.

The original Panopticon was the English philosopher Jeremy Bentham's model penitentiary. Bentham's idea was to construct a prison within which it would be possible, by means of rendering the prisoners' cells transparent to a central observation point, for the wardens to observe all the inmates all the time. Michel Foucault describes its function: "to induce in the inmate a state of conscious and permanent visibility that assures the automatic functioning of power. So to arrange things that the surveillance is permanent in its effects, even if it is discontinuous in its action." Such observations remind us how the modern state does not exercise power primarily through the overt deployment of force (the police officer's gun, the sheriff's eviction notice, the barbed wire atop the wall of the "correctional facility"), but through the *internalization* of its imperatives. A key element in this process of internalization is the juridical saturation of social space: the process by which all of us are made more or less continuously aware that we inhabit and move through a space full of legal and quasi-legal commands.

Indeed by comparison to Bentham's relatively modest scheme the modern panopticon's ambitions are almost unlimited: for although the inherent limitations of law ensure it will always be a rather crude social steering mechanism, this has not stopped the hypertrophied rationalism of modern legal thought from trying to bring more and more of human life under what it imagines to be law's benign gaze.

In contemporary America it often seems that everything not actually prohibited is required; indeed, as a practical matter many things are simultaneously prohibited *and* required. This curious paradox arises, in part, because of evidentiary problems and conceptual incommensurabilities that must plague any social coordination and dispute processing system. As we will see, such intractable problems ensure that attempts to create anything approaching a comprehensive legal regime must lead inevitably to such paradoxical outcomes.

Consider the following scenario: suppose I am an administrator at a state-sponsored law school. A male student begins wearing a T-shirt to class emblazoned with a vaguely political message that many other students, especially women, find disturbingly sexist and offensive. What can (must?) I do about this? The legal scholar Daniel Farber notes that such a situation will be governed initially by First Amendment "public forum" doctrines that divide public property into various different sorts of public forums, with different analytical tests relevant to the analysis of each one. Now as Farber points out, these multi-part tests are so notoriously vague and contradictory that it is widely acknowledged they can provide little real guidance to the harried administrator trying conscientiously to follow "the law." But this is just the beginning of the administrator's problems. For if one court decides, on whatever grounds, that the wearing of the shirt is a form of constitutionally protected conduct, another court in reviewing that judgment may well—given the vagueness of the relevant constitutional law doctrines—declare this same conduct to be not only unprotected but actually *illegal*, under equally vague civil rights law doctrines designed to protect the complaining students from a "hostile educational environment."

Farber's point is that these various legal "tests" are so amorphous that administrators can't determine with any real confidence whether they are required to intervene, are required *not* to intervene, or might even conceivably have some discretion in the matter. While certainly valid as far as it goes, this criticism doesn't address two deeper problems. First, Farber seems to assume it would be possible for the legal system to regulate this sort of social conflict in a more rational way by simply generating more determinate rules. But the vagueness of the rules isn't merely a product of bureaucratic arrogance and incompetence (which in any case are themselves in-eliminable factors in any complex system of dispute processing): that vagueness is also the unavoidable consequence of an essential tension between the clashing value systems—crudely speaking, between libertarian and communitarian norms—these rules are attempting to mediate. The rules are vague precisely because they are attempting to regulate conduct within what I will throughout this book refer to as an "equilibrium zone." Social, political, and legal equilibrium zones arise whenever public disputes implicate powerful competing ideological visions—visions that are themselves the products of axiomatic political and moral beliefs. Our fundamental beliefs about such matters are by their nature not amenable to rational analysis or disputation; indeed, as Richard Posner has pointed out, such beliefs must always "live below reason and are not the less worthy for doing so."

Second, as we will see in the next chapter, the competing ideological visions that always manifest themselves within social and political equilibrium zones can be counted on to produce both severe evidentiary problems and radically incommensurable conceptual understandings regarding the legal materials at issue. These in turn result in legal situations where it will literally be the case that, as a practical matter, a particular action will be both required and forbidden. Given the state of the relevant legal rules it is possible—and perhaps even probable—that in our hypothetical case the administrator will be found by a court to have violated the constitutional rights of the student for refusing initially to allow him to wear the shirt, and then will be held responsible by another court for violating the civil rights of the offended students by allowing the shirt to be worn.

So it isn't merely that the administrator is functioning in a social space where all freedom of action has been subverted by comprehensive juridical requirements. The deeper problem is that the rationalist goal of constructing comprehensive regulatory schemes designed to eliminate fundamental social conflict will lead inevitably to paradoxical overlaps and conceptual discontinuities in the official interpretation of those regulations. And those interpretive paradoxes will in turn produce absurd social situations in which *it is literally no longer possible* for even the most prudent, best-intentioned person to obey "the law."

The rationalist reaction to this dilemma is straightforward: keep doing what we're doing, only more so. Technocratic planners, totalizing social theorists, enthusiastic architects of new and better bureaucracies—all mimic the medieval barber whose response to a patient's deteriorating condition is always to open another vein.

Recently a well-known law professor wrote a review essay commenting on a book that took a dim view of the regulatory excesses and inefficiencies that characterize the modern administrative state. After admitting the author had made a number of telling points, the reviewer proceeded in the Pavlovian fashion of the doggedly helpful legal academic to suggest his own solution to this problem: an administrative agency that would promulgate regulations governing the promulgation of regulations by all other administrative agencies.

Such circumlocutions, immune as they are to parody, are degenerate heirs to the grand visions of the self-proclaimed "legal realists" who believed that law should shed what Felix Cohen called the "transcendental nonsense" of its conceptual metaphysics and replace formalist sophistry with the pursuit of rational technocratic planning.* The realist vision of law has since been elaborated on in a more overtly politicized vein by the critical legal studies movement, which for a brief time in the 1980s scandalized American law schools with a peculiar combination of intellectual audacity and new-left sloganeering, and which was responsible for the insight/ slogan "Law is politics." And although the idea critical legal studies meant to convey by that phrase is undoubtedly true—and is, moreover, true for all legal systems everywhere—this formula has inadvertently helped obscure a more local and hence more relevant insight, applicable especially to the present state of American law.

Politics Is Law

By the phrase "Law is politics," the critical legal studies movement meant to assert that all legal decisions were merely part of a special category of political decisions, and hence had to be justified on the basis of essentially political argument, rather than via formal deduction. The supposed neutrality of law was always a mask for a contingent and potentially controversial exercise of state power; and therefore particular exercises of that power could not be justified adequately on the self-referential grounds that the law required it.

---

*The logical conclusion of this train of thought was reached by Fred Rodell, a Yale Law School professor who has the dual distinction of producing the most apt comment ever made about legal academic writing ("There are two things wrong with almost all legal writing. One is its style. The other is its content."), and of authoring *Woe Unto You, Lawyers!*, described by Richard Posner as "the worst book ever written by a professor at a major law school." Rodell wanted to make the practice of law a crime, and to replace courts entirely with commissions of bureaucratic experts.

As one of the movement's gurus (Duncan Kennedy) put it, "there is never a correct legal solution to a problem that is other than the correct ethical and political solution to that legal problem." Now in a sense this statement seems self-evident. Who could have imagined that an institutionalized deployment of state power (law) could be justified on grounds that were not deeply parasitic on some more fundamental theory of political and moral obligation? The answer to this question, unfortunately, was "a large number of American legal academics." So in fact the critical legal studies movement performed a useful service by reminding legal thinkers that law always and everywhere is by necessity a specialized form of political action.

Yet this valuable insight has in its own way made it more difficult for legal thinkers to appreciate that the converse need not hold. There is no logical or practical reason why politics must be a specialized form of law. The denial of this assertion, however, may well be the central tenet of American legal ideology. The idea that political power is legitimate only to the extent this power is channeled through legal procedures, vocabularies, and modes of thought is such an integral part of both elite and popular American political culture that this idea might well be the key to what is meant by that obscure oracular phrase, "the rule of law." Indeed the eminent legal philosopher Ronald Dworkin has gone so far as to deny that ordinary interest group politics have *any* political legitimacy— unless, that is, the political compromises such groups reach can be made consonant with "a single, coherent set of principles," whose content must be determined by none other than federal judges. How these judges will manage to perform, in the course of sorting out the quotidian details of civil and criminal litigation, an intellectual feat that has eluded all political thinkers for several thousand years is left unexplained. Even more mysterious is the answer to the question of why anyone would believe that a group of civil service bureaucrats, whose professional education and experience has been focused on the interpretation of a necessarily parochial set of formal rules, would have any particular insight into such profound matters.

But Professor Dworkin is far from alone in his faith. Consider how Americans love to claim they hate politics, despise politicians, and loathe lawyers. Indeed, the most common insult hurled at those who address a question of public controversy is that they are "playing politics" with the issue. Of course on a superficial level this phrase merely means to assert that such persons are interested primarily in the aggrandizement of their own or their group's power, rather than in the merits of the issue itself. Yet the phrase's very ubiquity conveys a deeper cultural meaning. Accusing someone of "playing politics" can also be translated to mean something like "everyone knows what common sense and basic fairness require in this situation; you, however, are *politicizing* the issue, and thus contaminating it with ideological considerations, rather than simply advocating what everyone knows is the right thing to do."

Even relatively sophisticated venues for political argument often convey this particular subtextual message. A recent editorial in the highbrow opinion journal *The New Republic* condemned Bob Dole's proposed tax cut on the grounds that Dole's description of his proposal as comprising "a flatter, fairer tax" was "oxymoronic." Now an oxymoron is a statement that contains a logical contradiction. By contrast, we might define a "moron" as a person who believes questions involving matters of deep social controversy can be answered syllogistically.* After all, this would be true only if "everyone" "knew" that the major premise of such a logical argument was in fact correct. But of course the reason questions like these are matters of deep social controversy in the first place is that they can't be resolved by recourse to either logical or empirical argument. This inconvenient fact in turn reduces everyone to employing what appear to be rhetorically camouflaged emotive arguments, in the course of which "elementary logic," "the facts," "common sense," "public reason," and that perennial favorite "the Constitution" will

---

*That is, major premise: progressive tax rates are fairer than flatter tax rates; minor premise: Dole's plan calls for flatter, fairer taxes; conclusion: Dole's plan contains a logical contradiction. This reasoning is impeccable—as far as it goes.

all be enlisted in a doomed campaign to convince one's benighted opponents to see the error of their ways.

Americans hate politics because politics happen at just those junctures of social equilibrium where the invocation of such normative terms doesn't work. We can in a sense "prove" slavery is wrong by pointing to the social fact that there is no meaningful support for the idea that it isn't. This social fact can then be used to construct an apparently compelling argument that slavery is immoral. The uselessness of such insights for the resolution of live political controversies should be self-evident. Yet we remain entranced by the rationalist conceit that matters of deep political conflict are usefully amenable to rational argument. Hence we accuse those with whom we disagree of "playing politics" with important issues when, in all truth, what else could they (or we) do? Americans hate lawyers as well; in part because we pay lawyers to deny the intractable nature of significant political questions, which of course aggravates us no end when we find the lawyers on some side of an issue other than our own.

But—at least by comparison to their feelings for lawyers and politicians—Americans love judges. This should be quite a little mystery. After all judges are in essence nothing more than an especially politicized subclass of lawyers. The social role we give them requires judges to dispose of the most intractable social and political disputes by essentially arbitrary acts of fiat, while at the same time claiming their decisions are impelled by "the law" or "our constitutional traditions," or "fundamental rights inherent in the concept of ordered liberty," or some similar magic phrase.

And yet, despite intermittent moaning about judicial tyranny and government by judiciary, Americans show a remarkable tolerance for being sat on by this special class of bureaucratized politicians. To paraphrase Stalin, how many divisions do the courts have? The courts are lion tamers, with their flimsy chairs and ornamental whips, and the people are lions, who with a flick of a paw could obliterate their putative masters. Why then are we so docile? Is it the priestly robes? The obscurantist jargon? The sheer inertia that always underlies institutionalized authority? No doubt all these things play a part in maintaining the mass hypnosis that supports legal authority in general, and judicial power in particular, but we can also surmise more profound cultural tendencies are at work.

"Man cannot exist without bowing before something," wrote Dostoyevsky. "Let him reject God and he will bow before an idol." What Arthur Leff referred to as "the remarkably unappetizing idea" that "we are all we have" is something that unconsciously terrifies the votaries of the rule of law. Judges are the oracles of that cult; and the denial of their access to the special wisdom of the law—to whatever hidden lode of knowledge supposedly allows them to resolve profound political conflict without resort to raw social power— would require that we face up to the existential dread engendered by any cognizance of our true situation. This we are not going to do. Hence our willingness to allow matters of great public controversy to be jammed as a matter of course into the intellectually impoverished language of the law, with all its methodologically useless "three-part tests," its rationally inexplicable feats of "interest balancing," and its conclusory invocation of such god-terms as "legal principles," "substantial justice," and "the Constitution."*

Our public cultures feature many modes of legal faith, and many diverse sects worship at law's shrine. For example, nothing could be more inaccurate than the lazy assumption of the policy elites that groups such as the Freemen and the various militia movements represent anarchistic "anti-government" tendencies. If anything, the so-called anti-government forces of the radical right are among the

---

*"Many of [our] 'observations' are but implications of the particular terminology in terms of which the observations are made . . . perhaps the simplest illustration of this point is to be got by contrasting secular and theological terminologies of motives. If you want to operate, like a theologian, with a terminology that includes 'God' as its key term, the only sure way to do so is to put in the term, and that's that. The Bible solves the problem by putting 'God' into the first sentence—and from this initial move, many implications 'necessarily' follow . . . I have called metaphysics 'coy theology' because the metaphysician often introduces the term 'God' not outright, as with the Bible, but by beginning with a term that *ambiguously* contains such implications." Kenneth Burke, *Language as Symbolic Action*.

most fanatical devotees of legal authority among us. Indeed, near the end of their confrontation with the FBI (in what was always referred to as the "self-proclaimed" Township of Justus, a locution that surely suggests the question, "What other kind is there?") it was reported that the Freemen were worshipping the Constitution like an idol.

Such groups have elaborate ideological or rather theological justifications for the primacy of what they think of as the common law, the Constitution, and the inalienable rights of men. It is tempting to marginalize such persons as *merely* quasi-religious extremists; and some news accounts of the Freemen standoff tended to do did just that. Yet consider the broader implications of the following description, provided by Dr. J. Phillip Arnold, director of the Religion-Crisis Task Force in Houston, who as a specialist in extremist and apocalyptic religions was called on by the FBI to help end the confrontation. Arnold described the Freemen as an extremist religion for several reasons: they were willing to die for their beliefs; they were suspicious of outsiders; they possessed a sacred territory ("Justus Township"); they believed in sacred scripture, including the Bible, Magna Carta, Declaration of Independence, and United States Constitution; they recognized the higher authority of both God and their legal interpretations; and they conducted text-centered rituals, such as writing out writs, affidavits, and liens.

"Religion nowadays is a more expansive term than it was thirty years ago," Dr. Arnold explained. "There are some people who don't talk about God, Buddha, Jesus or the Bible, who are nevertheless religiously committed to an ideology." Indeed. This certainly can't be doubted by anyone who has ever seen American law professors pouring over every jot and tittle of the Constitution, searching for answers their faith tells them must lie amid the recondite symbols of that ever-changing, never-changing ancient text—answers that will reveal how, exactly, the most esoteric conflicts of our own day should be regulated. Is not some of the zeal of a righteous remnant also to be found among the contemporary talmudists of the ACLU, who *daven* furiously before their own secular decalogue and cry out that they shall have no gods before their God, the Bill of Rights? Words spoken in 1913, at the annual meeting of the Missouri Bar, merely confirm what all Americans know must be true, if the interpretation of our fundamental law is to rise above mere *politics*.

> Our great and sacred Constitution, serene and inviolable, stretches its beneficent powers over our land ... like the outstretched arm of God himself ... the people of the United States ... ordained and established one Supreme Court—the most rational, considerate, discerning, veracious, impersonal power—the most candid, unaffected, conscientious, incorruptible power ... O Marvelous Constitution! Magic Parchment! Transforming word! Maker, Monitor, Guardian of Mankind!*

We believe in the transcendent, more-than-human authority of "the rule of law," and by extension of its various fetish objects and their official interpreters, because the alternative would be to accept the authority of ourselves over ourselves. And that alternative, sadly, must remain so absurd as to represent a practical impossibility.

The Anarchic Panopticon

In C. S. Lewis's novel *Out of the Silent Planet* the protagonist Ransom, an English philologist, describes the earth's history of war, slavery, prostitution, and other evils to *sorns*, inhabitants of Mars. These beings are, like humans, *hnau*—rational creatures—who are under the rule of *eldila*, spirit-like entities analogous to earthly ideas of angels. The *sorns* are amazed by the wholesale moral corruption that marks human life, and speculate as to what might be its cause.

---

*I owe this quotation to Professor Henry Monaghan's fine essay, "Our Perfect Constitution," Vol. 56 *New York University Law Review*, p. 353 (1981). This verbal apotheosis gains a certain piquancy when we consider that, in the eighty-odd years since it was uttered, the constitutional interpretations undertaken by the rhapsode's "singularly rational and discerning Court" have not merely *altered* the meaning of "the" Constitution, but to a great extent have actually *inverted* it.

"They cannot help it," said the old *sorn*. "There must be rule, yet how can creatures rule themselves? Beasts must be ruled by *hnau* and *hnau* by *eldila* and *eldila* by Maleldil. These creatures have no *eldila*. They are like one trying to lift himself by his own hair—or one trying to see over a whole country when he is on a level with it—like a female trying to beget young on herself."

This passage is a nice description of the classic and perhaps insoluble problem of legal authority. "What is law," asks the legal philosopher Philip Soper, "that I should obey it?" Remarkably, there is a widespread consensus that this question—surely the most important question in the entire field of jurisprudence—has no satisfactory answer. The barriers to such an answer are both conceptual and practical. As a conceptual matter, it has proved very difficult to give any coherent description of what would even count as valid legal authority. For example, the classic political theories of the modern West usually rely on some concept of the consent of the governed when attempting to explain why legal directives are politically and ethically binding on those subject to them. But these accounts fail to explain adequately *why* consenting to legal rules obligates one to obey them. The theories either simply assert that people are obligated to keep their promises, or point to the general utilitarian benefits of promise keeping (which then raises the question of why should one always seek utility at the expense of other goods), or observe that, sociologically speaking, most people tend to believe they *are* obligated to keep their promises.

These unsatisfactory replies do not even address the most obvious objection to theories of consent, which is, of course, that as a matter of fact almost no one ever actually consents to being governed by a particular legal regime. This practical difficulty then leads to much intellectual wheel-spinning over theories of "tacit" or "implied" or "constructive" consent. Such flimsy fictions only point us toward the fundamental weakness of the whole concept of consent whenever it is invoked as a linchpin of liberal political theory. Think of it this way: did you "consent" to *any* of the most important circumstances of your life? To have these parents; to be brought up in this family; to be indoctrinated in this faith; to live in this neighborhood; to attend these schools; to be immersed in this culture; to be under the authority of this government, and all its multifarious legal obligations? By the time we get around to "freely consenting" to anything, we are in many ways no longer capable of doing so—at least not in that uncoerced manner in which the autonomous individual subject of classic liberal theory is supposed to assent to restrictions on his or her freedom.

And yet as an empirical matter, it remains the case that to the extent people believe in any account of legal obligation, they usually believe in some variation of the idea that it must be based on the consent of the governed. Thus other accounts of legal obligation— those that, for example, stress the importance of social coordination, or presume the existence of communities of principle or rational actors—face not only the empirical problem that society never actually resembles their accounts, but the further theoretical and practical difficulty that, unlike in the case of consent, almost no one accepts these equally problematic conceptual accounts as true.

Today our legal system faces an additional problem: the widespread acceptance of utilitarian modes of reasoning, which has produced a corrosive instrumentalism that ultimately undermines the very concept of binding authority. The frigid rationalisms of Jeremy Bentham and his followers have borne fruit in the idea that law is nothing but a matter of prudent self-interest; that, in the words of Joseph de Maistre, we are all merely members of a limited liability company, who obey certain communal directives for just so long as it remains in our mutual interest to do so. If the cultural myths and legal fictions that help maintain an essentially mystical belief in the authority of the state break down—if, in our society, it comes to be generally recognized that there is in fact no actual "social contract" —then law is reduced to a strategic, consequentialist practice: a complex exercise in game theory that binds no one and forbids nothing, unless it can be shown to be "useful" to pretend it does.

Hence our present condition: we all live in the midst of an *anarchic panopticon*. Bentham's rationalist dream whereby cadres of technocrats would maintain a continual surveillance of human behavior is being fulfilled—and not only in the penitentiary. "The law" is everywhere: yet increasingly, law is also nowhere at all. For if law is perceived as nothing but sets of rules deployed to pursue consequentialist purposes, then people will ignore or pervert those rules precisely to the extent necessary to get what they consider good results. At the level of crass self-interest this means that when, for instance, the government issues regulations requiring employers to provide family leave time, employees will duly "game" the rules, exploiting both ambiguities in their interpretation and unforeseen consequences flowing from their application to extract the maximum personal utility from the regulatory scheme. For their part, employers will react to this behavior by treating the regulations as incentives to corruption; and thus, rather than trying to follow the rules in good faith, they will attempt to limit the enforcement of those rules by every lawyerly stratagem at their disposal.

But the effects of corrosive instrumentalism are not limited to such obviously self-interested behavior. Once the concept of legal authority has begun to collapse—once the idea of doing what is required has been replaced by the goal of doing something else—then even actions born of the most altruistic motives will help produce essentially anarchic results. At present, the dominant generation of legal academics—law professors who were socialized in the heady days of the Warren Court—continually celebrate that court and its epigoni for sweeping aside petty considerations of positive law in order to do the right thing. But for legal decision makers "doing the right thing" soon becomes a habit they find difficult to break. That is, doing the right thing feels a little too good—so good that it becomes difficult to remember why, for example, a statute or a constitution isn't simply limited to some delightfully open-textured directive along the lines of "Do what substantial justice requires." (Indeed, typical examples of what is called "constitutional theory" indicate their academic authors might be surprised to discover the historical meaning of the U.S. Constitution is perhaps not *quite* identical with this particular phrase.)

Such ecstasies of jurisprudential righteousness help corrode the sense that the whole point of maintaining our enormous system of positive law, with its hundreds of millions of pages of text, entombing seemingly endless numbers of state and federal statutes, administrative regulations, executive orders, and, of course, the judicial opinions of fifty-one discrete jurisdictions, is to have some *law* out there that will at least decide a few things ahead of time. The contemporary American legal system thus often presents us with the perverse spectacle of historically unprecedented amounts of formal legal material being for the most part ignored by decision makers conditioned by the dominant ideology of the modern law school to act the part of the traditional Islamic *qaadi*, who was *supposed* to decide cases by "doing the right thing." The *qaadi*, however, wasn't burdened with the absurd task of sifting obsessively through a mountain of practically irrelevant formal materials before rendering what was understood to be a particular and pragmatic judgment. We on the other hand have managed to produce a legal system that both incurs all the costs of formal law, and allows the uncertainties of open-textured, particularistic judgment to eliminate most of the advantages of employing a formal dispute processing system.

"Man does not seek pleasure," wrote Nietzsche, "only the Englishman does." This characteristically elliptical aphorism points to the limitations that plague utilitarian accounts of human behavior. The structure of the anarchic panopticon helps reveal these limitations as well. For many purposes, law has been reduced to an instrumental, strategic practice in which considerations of valid legal authority play no real role; hence the inauthentic flavor of so much of the juridical saturation that pervades our lives. Much of the time, law is simply something we strive to exploit, avoid, or ignore. This, the modern panopticon's anarchic subtext, is a product of the failure of utilitarian visions of morality to create a genuine community of political and legal obligation. Yet the very fact of the panopticon's existence is also a testament to the enduring hunger for such a community; otherwise, why would such pragmatic people as Americans are reputed to be subject themselves to the obsessive excesses of the modern regulatory state, as well as to the pseudo-theological pretensions of their judicial priestcraft?

At this point in my argument I realize I am expected to follow certain conventions of legal academic writing. These require that, having given such an account of our situation, I rail at the intolerable dissonance and irrationality that plague our legal system, and demand we face our true circumstances without the comforting illusions that sustain the system's perceived legitimacy. Such at least is the rationalist conceit under which the modern academic labors. But what if it is the case that the practice of law, the practice of law teaching, and—especially—the practice of judging the law all to a significant degree require that we *not* perceive our actual situation? Is true knowledge really the goal—*should* it be the goal—of every discourse that claims to seek it? Perhaps the value intellectuals place on *talking about* the search for truth is more than a little analogous to the value football players put on the ability to bench press 500 pounds.

The maintenance of certain illusions may, after all, be more important than any Promethean insight the deliberative pursuit of truth might bring. As the old joke has it, a man goes to a psychiatrist and tells him that the man's brother thinks he is a chicken. When the psychiatrist asks the man why he doesn't bring his brother to him so that he can be cured of this disturbing delusion, the man replies, "I would, but I need the eggs." Let us at least hope our eggs will be laid by free-range chickens, gathered under humane conditions, and come to us both risk free and 100 percent guaranteed.

4

LEAVING LAS VEGAS

I have known what the Greeks did not: uncertainty.

JORGE LUIS BORGES, *The Lottery in Babylon*

A crowd of 150 men is gathered around a huge television screen, shouting at the top of its collective lungs. The scene is the sports book at a gigantic Las Vegas casino, the eponymous Mirage, and the occasion is the final minute of a college football game. Coming upon this display of unbridled passion a naive visitor assumes the contest must truly be hanging in the proverbial balance. He is in fact correct, but not in the sense he imagines.

The University of Nebraska is about to conclude another evisceration of a hapless opponent, and its coach, Dr. Tom Osborne (the Dr. Kevorkian of many a lesser colleague's career), has emptied his bench. The fourth-string quarterback, a walk-on from some wind-swept hamlet of the great plains, is lurching toward the goal line in what appears to be slow motion. If he should reach his goal, Nebraska's winning margin will swell to 49 points, sending precisely half the crowd into temporary ecstasy, and the other half into a slough of despond.

This seemingly strange ritual is a product of one of the most ingenious inventions of the American entrepreneurial mind: the gambling point spread. The point spread allows wagers on football and basketball games to be made at even odds, no matter how mismatched the respective teams might be. It works in the following way. Suppose that on a September weekend some college football powerhouse is scheduled to annihilate a sacrificial victim, which will for its trouble receive a nice paycheck. Gambling emporiums then duly establish a "line," a number that they estimate will produce an equal number of bets on each team. Let us say the number is Nebraska minus 43. This means that for the gambler with his money on Nebraska to collect on his bet, the vaunted Cornhuskers must win the game by more than 43 points. Conversely, if he places his money on the underdog, the sacrificial victim must not lose by more than 43 points. It is an even money bet, with the house keeping a percentage of the winning wagers—usually around 10 percent —that covers its costs, generates profit, and ensures mathematically that in the long run the gamblers lose and the casino wins.

The beauties of this scheme are several. First, the line makes for much more lively betting than a variable odds system, especially when, as is often the case in college sports, the contest is a mismatch. A 43-point spread correlates with something like a 250–1 chance for the underdog to win outright. That is a fundamentally uninteresting bet to the serious sports gambler: at those odds, he might as well buy a lottery ticket. On the other hand an even money proposition always generates the greatest gambling interest among the cognoscenti, as it by definition reflects a perfect balance of informed opinion concerning the question at hand.

Second, the line will more often than not result in a contest that remains, in the relevant sense, in some doubt until its final moments. This feature explains those otherwise puzzling spectacles of passionate intensity produced by the continuing presence of the wagering interest, when all other interest in the game has long since departed. It has been noted that despite—or perhaps because of— eons of efforts by stern moralists, people will bet on quite literally anything if given half the chance. Indeed there is no activity that can't be made utterly fascinating by the simple expedient of wagering on its outcome. Combine this with the natural interest most men in this culture feel regarding the outcome of sporting events, and the pretensions they (all right, we) harbor regarding our expertise in such matters, and the sheer genius of the line becomes all the more apparent.

Third, and most germane to the topic of this book, the line is a marvelously elegant demonstration of the power and the limitations of both individual and collective rationality. For the line is not stable: it shifts in reaction to the ongoing wagers made around it. Suppose that Nebraska "opens" as a 17-point favorite against Kansas. This again is an estimate on the part of the house as to what number will split the betting evenly. The betting public then displays a small but significant preference for Kansas; the line moves to 16, and then to 15 1/2. Finally it stabilizes, as the action comes in at equal proportions for both teams. Much of the time the house's initial estimate of the matter is so accurate that the line moves not at all. In either case, this collective judgment often predicts with a seemingly diabolical accuracy the actual outcome of the contest; and always, for any statistically significant number of games, the favorites and the underdogs will each "cover the spread" almost exactly half the time.

The foregoing account will come as no surprise to anyone who is familiar with the behavior of financial markets. Such markets are in effect sports books on an exalted economic and social scale, and the classic account of their behavior, the so-called "efficient market theory," predicts precisely the outcomes I describe above. The efficient market theory comes in several versions, making claims of varying strength. I will therefore first describe the theory at a general level, before noting specific disagreements regarding what version mostly closely correlates with the structure of American financial markets.

More than forty years ago, the statistician Maurice Kendall noticed that fluctuations in stock prices appeared to follow what is called a "random walk." A random walk is a statistical pattern in which previous iterations of a phenomenon have no predictive value regarding its future course. In other words stock price fluctuations seemed to follow no predictable pattern. With some unimportant— i.e., non-exploitable—exceptions, Kendall's observations have proven correct. Indeed, Richard Brealey and Stewart Myers note that "with remarkable unanimity researchers have concluded that there is no useful information in the sequence of past changes in stock price. As a result, many of the researchers have become famous. None has become rich."

At first, the random-walk pattern of stock prices was met with surprise. Yet it soon became apparent that this empirical outcome should have been anticipated theoretically; and in fact it *was* anticipated, at the turn of the century, in an obscure doctoral thesis by a French writer, Louis Bachelier. Armed with these initially puzzling facts, economists determined that a random walk is exactly what one should expect in the prices of an efficiently functioning financial market. They reasoned that in a competitive market that processes information efficiently, investments will achieve an equilibrium price. An equilibrium price is a price that incorporates and therefore reflects all the relevant information available to investors. Brealey and Myers sum up why price changes in an efficient market must be random:

> If prices always reflect all relevant information, then they will change only when new information arrives. But new information *by definition* cannot be predicted ahead of time (otherwise it would not be new information). Therefore stock prices cannot be predicted ahead of time. To put it another way, if stock prices reflect all that is predictable, then stock price changes must reflect only the unpredictable.

Analysts disagree as to just how efficient various financial markets actually are. In its weak form, the efficient price theory holds that stock prices reflect all information contained in the record of past prices. Almost all researchers agree that American financial markets are efficient in this sense. A stronger version of the theory declares that current prices also reflect all "published" or "public" information (e.g., earnings and dividend announcements, forecasts of future earnings, predictions of mergers, etc.). Although one would guess that significant problems exist at the margin when attempting to determine what information is truly public, Brealey and Myers nevertheless note that "the price reaction to [such] news appears to be almost immediate," and that "most of this information [is] rapidly and accurately impounded in the price of the stock," making the potential gain from the information less than the transaction cost of acting on it. It appears the majority of analysts believe—subject to various caveats—that American financial markets are efficient in this stronger sense. Finally, the strongest version of the theory holds that stock prices reflect *all* the relevant information an investor could hope to acquire about a stock. This version would seem to be contradicted empirically by the successful practice of "insider" trading, and refuted theoretically by the undeniable presence of information and trading costs (the strongest form of the theory requires these costs to be zero). Hence there is almost no support for the strong version of the theory, although Brealey and Myers note it should give us pause that studies of professionally managed portfolios have concluded that, after factoring in risk, "no group of institutions have been able to outperform the market consistently and that even the differences between the performance of individual funds are no greater than you would expect from chance."

Let us return to the Mirage sports book so as to concretize these observations in a more glamorous setting. How efficient are betting markets? To answer this question, we need only review the process that creates the betting line. Recall that the setting of a line is a two-step process: first, the sports book sets an initial number, which then fluctuates in response to the bets that are made. We might ask as an initial matter how it is that bookmakers are able to predict with such accuracy the betting public's reaction to a particular line, and why that reaction itself so closely correlates with the outcome of any significant set of games. The answers to these questions bring us face to face with both the power and the limitations of rational inquiry.

In the season of mists and mellow fruitfulness I will sometimes annoy my wife into participating in a childish game called "guess the line." She consults the betting line printed in the local newspaper (along with a spurious disclaimer, "for entertainment purposes only" —law *is* everywhere) and has me estimate the line on various pro and college football games. Although I give each question perhaps five seconds consideration, around two-thirds of the time I am able to come within a point or two of the actual spread and I am rarely off by more than three. This trivial accomplishment is the combined product of a no doubt unhealthy level of interest in football and the somewhat—but not completely—predictable nature of the game itself. Now I don't doubt that my modest abilities in this regard pale before the expertise and perspicacity of a professional bookmaker;

nevertheless they may give us some glimpse into how those more accomplished persons go about their task.

Suppose I am trying to determine what the spread will be on the upcoming Colorado–Michigan college football game. Colorado is ranked fifth in the nation, Michigan tenth. I sense, with that inchoate but generally accurate sense of these things serious fans possess, that as a consequence of their national reputations both teams are a little overrated by casual observers (i.e., sportswriters), Michigan perhaps a bit more so. On a neutral field, I would make Colorado about a six point favorite, but since the game is in Boulder I would bump that to nine, maybe ten points. When I look in the paper next week, I will be very surprised if a few hundred thousand serious bettors haven't analyzed the game in much the same way. After all, with almost no important exceptions we have the same information to work with, and roughly the same set of experiences in regard to the significance of similar information in the past. It therefore isn't surprising that we come to very similar conclusions; what would be surprising would be if we didn't. Such is the nature of the competitive rational analysis of potentially valuable public information: among serious competitors, disagreement will only begin to take place in that zone of analytic equilibrium where the absence of information and the presence of randomizing effects are much more important factors than whatever marginal differences exist in the interpretive abilities of the competitors.

This is not to say that serious bettors have *all* the relevant information. Of course they don't: they probably won't know that Michigan's quarterback is breaking up with his girlfriend, or perhaps even that Colorado's best player twisted his knee in practice. But note that to the extent this information becomes public they will all assimilate it—tacitly, perhaps even unconsciously, but quite efficiently all the same. And given the tremendous incentives to acquire relevant information, it is probable that the more important the piece of information, the more likely it will become known to the betting public.

The betting line thus functions as a highly accurate equilibrium price that establishes successfully the collective investment value of all individual bets: zero minus the transaction cost of the wager. A simple example: if I bet $50 on Nebraska giving $15\frac{1}{2}$ points, there will be in an efficiently functioning betting pool a .5 probability of Nebraska winning by more than 15 points, in which case I will be up $50 minus the bookmaker's fee, and a .5 probability of their winning by less than 16 points or losing outright, in which case I will be down $50. And on the basis of both theoretical modeling and experimental evidence, there is every reason to believe that public betting lines price their products just as efficiently as financial markets price theirs. Thus in the long run the bookie must win and the gambler must lose.

Nevertheless, compulsive gamblers often indulge in the illusion that if they could only get their hands on the "inside story," they could beat the betting line and make the killing that will get them even. But the inside story rarely exists, or, more precisely, the real inside story isn't something even the best informed gamblers can get at. Of course occasionally people do acquire really valuable inside information: just ask Ivan Boesky or, if you can get through to base-ball hell, Joe Jackson.* But what makes both betting and investing interesting is that even with the best possible information a person could reasonably hope to acquire, a large amount of what affects the fortunes of companies and football teams can't be learned ahead of time and is therefore practically inaccessible to the investor, or indeed is truly random, and hence isn't predictable even in theory. Rational analysis, especially when a communal structure of inquiry negates idiosyncratic predilections, goes a long way toward producing true knowledge. But it can't go all the way, because some of the necessary information is either as a practical matter unknowable in advance or—and here we touch on the mysterious element in the concept of the random—isn't knowable at all.

The power of reason is evident in the fact that I can in five sec-

---

*Although even in the case of the Black Sox scandal of 1919, which remains the only authenticated instance of a major American professional team sport contest being "fixed," the knowledge of the impending fix became so common so quickly that even some of the fixers were unable to profit from it.

onds make a roughly accurate prediction of the outcome of a football game and an extremely accurate prediction of other people's
predictions of the same thing. The limitations of rational inquiry are
manifested by the fact that, leaving aside the possibility of new
information becoming available, I could study the same questions
for a week and have little or no chance of answering them more
accurately. Appreciating the significance of such facts leads to the
counterintuitive insight that, in an efficient process of collective reasoning, the employment of reason works to make its further
employment unreasonable. In other words, the investment of *intellectual* capital and labor is just as subject to problems of diminishing
marginal utility as is the investment of their better understood
material cousins. This is precisely why people buy shares in cheap,
market-indexed mutual funds, rather than paying someone to try
and beat the market, or attempting to do so themselves. Yet the
notion that, in the long run, it is possible for gifted individuals to
analyze the information relevant to a system of competitive rational
analysis in such a way as to achieve significantly better results than
those achieved by the collective reason of the process itself remains
one of the most tenacious illusions of rationalism.*

So tenacious is this illusion that whole industries of rationalist
divination—investment counseling guides, gambling tip sheets,
appellate court decisions—sustain themselves within the ambit of its
hypnotic glow. I now turn to the latter of these phenomena.

---

*What about George Soros, Warren Buffett, the ladies' guild that beat the market
by 20%, and so on? If 10,000 people each flip a coin ten times, and five of them get
"heads" on all ten attempts, this isn't evidence of a special ability. If fifty were to do
so, that would be another matter. In both financial and wagering markets extraordinary returns on investment are achieved by individuals at levels consistent with
expected patterns of random statistical deviation from the mean. Thus even if we
were to assume certain individuals have the ability to "beat the market," the statistical
fact this does not happen any more often than would occur by simple chance means
that, for the purposes of *institutional* decision making, such extraordinary abilities—if
indeed they exist—have no practical significance. When taking part in a process of
collective reasoning it is better to be lucky than good; or rather, in an efficient market, those concepts will amount to the same thing.

The Efficient Process Theory

I live in a typical American small town of about 15,000 people. Every day, literally millions of events take place here that could in theory be the subject of formal legal action. Every time someone buys a loaf of bread, writes a check, borrows a car, turns up the stereo, waters the lawn, gets into an argument, or takes care of a neighbor's pet, those actions are subject to the possibility of formal legal intervention; indeed, the list could fill this entire book and yet be far from complete. Of course in only a minuscule percentage of these cases will it ever occur to anyone, however fleetingly, that such action could or should take place; and it will in turn be in only a tiny proportion of *those* instances where some such action ever comes about.

This in itself should not be surprising. We don't normally think about the legal ramifications of our actions for the same reason a man never thinks about his liver until it begins to bother him: laws, like livers, are invisible when they are working as they should.

Almost every feature of the educational and cultural indoctrination law students undergo conspires to make them forget this simple point. In the American law school, the focus of pedagogical inquiry, and indeed the very site of "the law" itself, is almost invariably the appellate court opinion. And what are these opinions? Consider how for every dispute that ripens into even the possibility of a lawsuit or an arrest, millions of frictionless legal transactions take place, most of them blissfully free of any conscious knowledge on the part of the participants that they are in any sense partaking in legal interaction. For every dispute involving some sort of formal legal action, there are dozens of conflicts where such action was considered but were resolved without recourse to it. For every civil lawsuit resulting in a formal courtroom disposition, there are between thirty and fifty suits that are settled prior to this point. And for every lower court disposition of a case that results in an appellate court opinion, there are many more that do not.

Imagine a volcanic island whose base is thirty miles wide, and rises out of waters 35,000 feet deep. The portion of the island above water is only 200 feet in diameter, and the highest patch of this ground is but 20 feet above sea level (this is roughly what the island of Hawaii would look like if the Pacific were 13,000 feet deeper at the spot where it emerges from the sea). On this patch of ground lies a single stone, about the size of a baseball. The submerged portion of this island represents the invisible workings of the law when it functions as a successful medium of social coordination. The portion above the water represents the visible world of formal legal action. The stone represents the universe of appellate court cases. Lawyers, law students, and especially legal academics routinely mistake that stone for an entire island, and then name it "law."

Why is almost the entire island of law submerged from view? Formal legal action takes place for many reasons: because of disagreements about the facts of a social interaction; because of a fundamental conflict of moral views; because the relevant rules are ambiguous, contradictory, anachronistic, or otherwise controversial; because people are willing to spend money to sublimate their emotions into public modes of expression; and many other reasons as well. Given how we all tend to notice the presence of something more readily than its absence, we rarely appreciate that on the vast majority of occasions, none of these various preconditions for overt legal action is present. And even when one or more of these factors is present, it is much more likely than not that the absence of other factors will keep the dispute from going into a formal legal orbit.

Suppose I ask you on a Monday if I can borrow your car for the next week. You say "sure," when what you mean, naturally enough, is "unless I need it back for some really pressing reason." On Friday you learn you have an opportunity to use a friend's seaside summer house for the coming weekend. You need your car to get there, so you walk over to my place. Once there, you find the car parked on the street and that I'm not home, so you leave a note explaining why you're taking the car before driving off with it. Now I may get quite angry at you. I may believe we had a "deal." I may even think of you as a morally defective person for acting in this way. But if I should be so rash as to consult a lawyer, I will be told that I don't have any grounds for legal complaint because, as a matter of fact, I don't.

This is the portion of the island of law near the island's shoreline: that becomes visible, as it were, when the tidal pull of social coordination is low. Most of the time, of course, such interactions don't lead to open conflict of any sort, and such conflicts that do take place never reach a lawyer's office. The island remains almost completely underwater.

The key to understanding what I will call "the efficient process theory" is this: law becomes present to us through its absence. Conversely, law's very presence tends to negate our perception of that presence. This is a fancy Hegelian phrasing of the same idea behind the baseball truism that says you never notice the umpires when they're doing their job right. (As Yogi Berra is reputed to have observed, "All I ever really needed to know about phenomenology I learned from sports.")

The efficient process theory consists of the following propositions.

1) In a legal system, efficiently processed disputes will be settled to the extent that the available information predicts a likely outcome.

This follows from the obvious point that, subject to exceptions for disputes being processed for reasons other than to advance directly the interests of the litigants, rational litigants will pursue or defend against an action until they have achieved a sufficient level of confidence concerning what the probabilities for the final outcome of the dispute seem to be. Once this point is reached, processing the dispute further merely increases the transaction costs incurred in the course of resolving it. A dispute is thus "efficiently processed" when it remains in the dispute processing system only until enough information becomes available to make a sufficiently accurate estimate concerning its eventual outcome.

Consider two relatively pure examples. The first case is our hypothetical car loan between friends. The legal system processes this dispute so efficiently that a lawyer can immediately inform me of the value of undertaking legal action: zero minus transaction costs. And since even if I'm not a lawyer I'm likely to have a tacit appreciation of that fact, this dispute is likely to remain completely "below the surface," part of the vast invisible island of law. By contrast, assume the lawyers processing a dispute become certain, given their analysis of the formal rules, the evidence, the judge, the jury, their overall situation sense, and whatever else they believe relevant, that the jury will return a verdict of $100,000 for the plaintiff. The present value of the dispute to the plaintiff is then $100,000 minus whatever transaction costs the plaintiff has already incurred, while to the defendant the dispute has a value of minus $100,000, plus sunk transaction costs. Assuming both parties are in a position to incur equivalent future costs by continuing the dispute, and assuming that (not coincidentally) it is both the lawyers' professional obligation and in their long-term economic interests to maximize their clients' welfare, the case will then settle for $100,000.

Of course whenever they deal with the visible rather than the invisible law, lawyers will never be certain of anything to this extent. But the point of the ideal case is to illustrate that *to the extent* the dispute process moves the disputants toward certainty, the process moves toward resolution. This analysis is undoubtedly far too neat and formalistic, and we should not take it too literally. But the theoretical point is surely valid: in general, to the extent people can predict legal outcomes they will avoid engaging in formal legal disputes, either by avoiding them altogether or terminating them as soon as the dispute process reveals a sufficiently predictable set of likely results. In other words, the more clearly the information made available by the dispute process predicts a particular outcome, the sooner the dispute will be terminated, while conversely, to the extent the process fails to produce a reliable prediction, the further the dispute will tend to travel through the dispute processing system. This brings us to the theory's second proposition.

2) The further an efficiently processed dispute travels through a dispute processing system, the more firmly that dispute is lodged in a legal equilibrium zone.

A legal equilibrium zone is a sort of negative analogue to an "equilibrium price," that is, to whatever stock price incorporates and reflects all the relevant information available to investors, thereby allowing the stock to be valued accurately. Whatever factors the dispute processing system considers relevant to the resolution of the dispute—formal rules, inchoate cultural norms, local knowledge of the system, the wealth or status of the disputants—is by definition relevant information. Therefore whatever the system considers, formally or informally, in the processing of the dispute (and whether we call this mass of material "law," or "principle," or "politics," or "social power," or something else altogether makes no difference to the analysis) is in equilibrium to the extent that the state of this material makes it difficult or impossible to predict how the dispute will be resolved. A dispute is thus in an equilibrium zone when its travels through the dispute processing system have not yet provided the disputants with enough information to allow them to make a sufficiently accurate estimate of the dispute's eventual outcome.

Naturally, the disputes that will prove hardest to move out of legal equilibrium zones will be those in which whatever considerations the broader culture considers most important remain in the greatest tension: in other words, those legal disputes taking place in what in the previous chapter I described as *social* and *political* equilibrium zones. These will be disputes in which, for example, powerful moral claims of an axiomatic and even mystical nature—in our culture claims regarding concepts such as "equality," "liberty," "personhood," "fairness," and so forth—seem to be irreconcilably at odds. Conflicts that feature a clash between what appears to be justice in the individual case and the consistent enforcement of general norms or conflicts in which it is claimed that important interests of some members of the community must be sacrificed for what seems like the good of the many will also fit this model.

One result of these various interpretive tensions is that the outcome of many legal disputes will turn on conceptually incommensurable definitions of what "the law" is. Indeed, the American legal system's tacit toleration of such interpretive incommensurability helps ensure the "same" piece of law will be capable of accommodating contradictory answers to especially difficult legal questions. Consider a simple, very common example of this phenomenon. Suppose that while the so-called "plain" (literal, apparent, at-first-glance) meaning of a statute's language appears to produce a clear rule for dealing with a certain dispute, a more fully contextualized interpretation of that language reveals the enacting legislature intended a different rule, one perhaps better suited to what the interpreter considers justice in a particular case. Now, is the meaning of a statute determined by what the legislature that passed it thought it meant, or by what the statute's language would be taken to mean, at first or second glance, by some hypothetical ordinary observer? (As the reader can anticipate, the answer our legal system gives to this interpretive question is "yes.")

Here we should note an important difference between, on the one hand, dispute processing systems, and on the other, financial and wagering markets. In the latter cases, there is little ambiguity about what kind of evidence is relevant to a rational prediction of what the systems in question will do, because there is little controversy about what the point of the respective activities is—predicting which team will win by how much, and which corporations will be more or less profitable. By contrast, most difficult legal problems involve not only complicated empirical questions, but also problematic judgments concerning questions of moral value, and (often as a direct consequence of these other difficulties) various conceptually incommensurable definitions of what sorts of facts are said to constitute legal meaning. These latter types of disputes will tend not to be amenable to resolution through the procurement of more evidence via the workings of the dispute processing system, either because they involve conceptual disagreements about what should even count as evidence, or because they can't usefully be thought of as involving evidentiary questions at all. But even more prosaic legal questions may prove intractable if the evidence the system needs to process the dispute toward a predictable outcome is too difficult or expensive to procure. Thus a corollary of the theory's second proposition is that in a system that processes disputes efficiently, disputes will travel through the system until they emerge from an equilibrium zone, or until the costs of attempting to make them do so become too high. A second corollary is that when either point is reached, the process terminates. This brings us to our theoretical conclusion:

3) In an efficient dispute processing system the terminal decision making structures of the system will resolve disputes arationally.

This conclusion is profoundly inimical to rationalist ideology in general, and to American legal thought in particular. Indeed, it would be fair to say the conventional view of how law works is precisely the opposite of the conclusion reached here. The celebrated political philosopher John Rawls is in his own grandiloquent way speaking not only for himself, but for whole academic disciplines, political ideologies, and pervasive social institutions when he asserts that "in a constitutional regime with judicial review, public reason is the reason of its supreme court." (For Rawls, "public reason" is that exercise of rational decision making that makes political decisions legitimate.) On a similar note, Mary Ann Glendon of the Harvard Law School has recently described the proper exercise of legal thought toward the solution of difficult legal questions as a kind of "singing reason," and Dean Anthony Kronman has characterized his Yale Law School, which with Harvard supplies the lion's share of elite American lawyers to the bar, the bench, and the academy, as a "community united by faith in the power of reason." It would be putting it mildly to say a conclusion that the role of reason in legal argument is to render itself superfluous will not prove congenial to our legal elites.

If, as Richard Posner has asserted, a pragmatic as opposed to a formalist conception of law is damaging to the *amour propre* of the legal profession, what reaction can we expect to an explicitly anti-rationalist approach? But my argument is not attempting, in the neurotic style of so much academic discourse, to *convince* people whose professional identities are invested in the conceptual scheme the argument attacks. I merely aim to *convert* them.*

Disturbing as the argument might be, its conclusion is logically entailed by what has gone before. Indeed, once one has given up on the dogma that there must be rationally determinable answers to difficult legal issues, the question becomes how people can believe disputes that have reached the terminal decision-making point in a legal system *are* generally amenable to yet more extensive rational analysis. If the relevant materials allow the disputants to predict with confidence the outcome of a rational analysis of a dispute, why do they continue to incur processing costs? Of course people occasionally value engaging in the process for reasons other than pursuing the formal disposition of their dispute per se, as when, for instance, what they seek is to have their view heard in a formal public setting, or when they derive satisfaction from the conflict itself. But relative indifference to the practical outcome of litigation on the part of the litigant is as rare as indifference to the outcome of a bet on the part of the bettor, or to the fluctuation of a stock on the part of the investor. In all these cases the practical outcome of the process is almost always the paramount consideration.

Thus if lawyers persist in processing disputes whose outcomes are usefully amenable to rational analysis—i.e., disputes whose outcomes will be sufficiently predictable to allow them to be valued

---

*One of the unwarranted conceits of rationalism is that it is possible to convince people through the sheer persuasive force of reasoned argument to discard their most basic worldviews:

> May someone have telling grounds for believing the earth has only existed for a short time, say since his own birth?—Suppose he had always been told that,— would he have any good reason to doubt it? Men have believed they could make rain; why should not a king be brought up in the belief that the world began with him? And if [G. E.] Moore and this king were to meet and discuss, could Moore really prove his belief to be the right one? I do not say that Moore could not convert the king to his view, but it would be a conversion of a special kind; the king would be brought to look at the world in a different way.

Ludwig Wittgenstein, *On Certainty*, paragraph 92.

accurately for the purposes of rational resolution—one of two conclusions must follow.

1. Lawyers pursue such disputes because increasing the transaction
costs of processing disputes is ultimately in their interest. This claim
is belied by the observation that a lawyer's interests are in the long
run dependent on the pursuit of the interests of his or her clients.
Lawyers who incur unnecessary costs for their clients are putting
themselves at a systematic competitive disadvantage with lawyers
who do not. Indeed, dispute processing systems that incur too many
avoidable costs will put themselves at a disadvantage with alternative
systems that avoid doing so. It is therefore in the long-term interest
of both individual lawyers and the system as a whole to resolve
clients' disputes as soon as there is enough information available to
allow them to do so with confidence.

This theoretical observation is buttressed by the empirical fact
that for every appellate court decision, there are thousands of cases
that never get that far in the formal legal system. Indeed, for every
formally filed case, there are several disputes that lawyers help settle
without taking formal legal action of any kind. Of course some
number of corrupt, desperate, or ideologically driven ("the cause is
more important than my client") lawyers will convince their clients
to continue the pursuit of cases whose outcomes have become eminently predictable. But if this sort of thing is in fact commonplace, it
is no refutation of the efficient process theory. On the contrary, it
merely confirms that the system in question is not an efficient dispute processing system. This then leaves us with an alternative
explanation:

2. The lawyers who pursue such disputes do so because they, unlike
the lawyers who decide the disputes, lack the requisite cognitive
skills to subject the disputes in question to successful rational analysis.

This claim comes down to saying that judges, and especially legal
academics (who, as Pierre Schlag has pointed out, have traditionally
imagined themselves to be the judges of the judges), are just smarter
than lawyers in general. Actually the claim is much more audacious

than that. The claim must be that judges and law professors are *so much* smarter than other lawyers that their exceptional ability to analyze otherwise intractable disputes enables them to succeed *as a matter of professional routine* at the task of moving such disputes squarely out of interpretive equilibrium zones and into the realm of the sufficiently predictable outcome.

The philosopher John Searle has noted, in the course of describing various incredible claims about the nature of human consciousness, that "people who are about to say something that sounds silly very seldom come right out and say it. Usually a set of rhetorical or stylistic devices is employed to avoid having to say it in words of one syllable." So it is in law. Indeed such devices are the lawyer's bread and butter. Thus you are unlikely to come across judges or judge-wanna-bes who say things such as "the people who are arguing so passionately about this apparently intractable legal, moral, and political issue are just too dumb to see the answer." Instead, they tend to say things like this:

> [Issues such as abortion], involving the most intimate and personal choices a person may make in a lifetime, choices central to personal dignity and autonomy, are central to the liberty protected by the Fourteenth Amendment. At the heart of liberty is the right to define one's own concept of existence, of meaning, of the universe, and of the mystery of human life. Beliefs about these matters could not define the attributes of personhood were they formed under compulsion of the state.
>
> [*Planned Parenthood v. Casey*]

This is supposed to address the question of whether or not states are legally entitled to regulate abortion. (By the way, the answer this judicial opinion eventually gives, after more than 100 pages of equally helpful analysis, is "sort of.") The rhetorical tricks involved —begging the question in extremely abstract, oracular language and then proceeding to assert a non sequitur—are not very edifying, although familiar enough to any lawyer. What is remarkable is how this kind of thing can send otherwise discerning persons into analytic ecstasy:

The Joint Opinion see[s] in the citizen a capacity for responsible tension and growth, [and sees] in the process of law— especially in the work of the [Supreme] Court—a source of education for itself and the polity.... The conversation to which the Joint Opinion is committed is the direct descendent of that to which Socrates was committed, which he would rather die than damage, the conversation that assumes that Athens, or America, is a moral actor with a moral career, capable of justice or injustice.

If one can somehow keep a grip on what *Planned Parenthood v. Casey* actually is—the bureaucratic work product of twentysomething judicial clerks, whose relevant life experience consists for the most part in getting good grades and otherwise ingratiating themselves with various authority figures—one is tempted to conclude that the eminent professor who penned this encomium had lost his mind. How wholesome, by contrast, seems Oliver Wendell Holmes' philosophically modest observation that he considered a law constitutional unless it made him want to "puke." Granted, the puke test lacks analytic content, but who other than a few self-deluded ideologues thinks that issues such as the morality of abortion can be resolved through the successful employment of what they call "reason?*"

The efficient process theory holds that what is true for abortion is true generally for disputes that go to the terminal points of an efficiently functioning legal system. If this theory is correct, then the appellate judge who thinks "the law" gives him the answer to an efficiently processed legal question is in the grip of a rationalist delusion. Legal equilibrium zones are produced by profound tensions and uncertainties in the interpretive materials with which lawyers

---

*"The idea that even the most passionate political and ideological disagreements rest on mere analytic errors is the faith of a certain kind of analytic philosopher ... none of the weapons in the armory of the analytic philosopher or expert legal reasoner will or should deflect a person who believes that the fetus is a human being and the abortionist a murderer. Those beliefs, like other fundamental beliefs, live below reason and are not the less worthy for doing so." Richard Posner, *Overcoming Law*, p. 188.

and judges must work: tensions and uncertainties that mirror intractable conflicts between the various explicit and tacit social norms these materials reflect. Thus the so-called "realist" view held by many modern legal scholars—that when what they think of as "law" fails to provide an answer to a difficult legal question a recourse to "policy" or "politics" will help—can be sustained only if there is some reason to think the rational analysis of difficult political and moral questions will be more successful than the analysis of difficult "legal" questions. But once we appreciate that difficult legal questions *are* difficult because they implicate, directly or indirectly, rationally undecidable political and moral disputes, we will be less prone to make this same mistake.

We can now better appreciate why law becomes present to us through its absence. For it is in just those situations where law is going to fail to give us answers that we will be most insistent that it do so. The intensity of our concerns about what the law requires will therefore tend to correlate inversely with the presence of clear legal requirements; and our pleas to judges to exercise "good judgment" will take place in just those circumstances where good judgment isn't going to help either them or us.

Indeed the efficient process theory suggests the following inversion of conventional legal thought: what lawyers refer to as "frivolous" cases will often be those disputes that we recognize as having been inefficiently processed *precisely because* we recognize that, although these cases *are* usefully amenable to rational evaluation, they have nevertheless approached the terminal point in the formal dispute processing system. Thus the frivolous case isn't the case that isn't worth thinking about, but rather the opposite. Paradoxically, it is the serious dispute in which the extensive employment of reason ends up being an exercise in rationalist frivolity.

Leaving Las Vegas

Is American law an efficient dispute processing system? This deceptively simple question requires a somewhat complex answer. Consider two institutions of the American legal process: the voting booth and the jury. Voting, whether in a legislative or a directly democratic setting, is an explicitly arational mechanism for deciding controversial issues. Hardly anyone thinks that the appropriate way to determine whether a meteorite in Antarctica holds evidence of life on Mars is to ask for a general show of hands. But it is just as ridiculous to imagine that one can determine successfully whether a fetus has a right to life by consulting supposed experts on that question, whether these be scientists, moral philosophers, platonic guardians, or the politicized lawyers called judges. In this sort of legal, moral, and political equilibrium zone the putative reasons given for deciding to do this rather than that are ultimately post-hoc rationalizations, designed to justify axioms and intuitions that are not worth arguing about. Like all such beliefs, the axioms and intuitions that make up the basis of one's own moral reasoning are not and indeed cannot be open to either real examination or self-reflective critique. They are what Holmes, that great skeptic among American judges, called his "can't helps."

When deciding what to do about such questions it is eminently rational to refuse to engage in rational analysis. Voting is thus a sensible way to resolve conflicts of value precisely because it doesn't require any justification of particular results beyond reference to the formal definition of the activity itself. ("Why did we adopt this rule? Because more people voted for it.")

At bottom many judges and most legal theorists dislike democracy because it is an implicit acknowledgment of the severe limitations of their expertise. Among legal academics, the formalist wants the immanent rationality of the law to decide deep conflicts of value, while the realist wants to put a commission of technocrats in charge of such questions, and the critical scholar strives to politicize the masses so as to rid them of the false consciousness he thinks causes the conflicts in the first place. The moral and intellectual pretensions of judges are more troubling, if only because they have discernible consequences. So it is that in America today it has become possible to produce a document such as the joint plurality opinion in *Planned Parenthood v. Casey*, which permits persons of the modest jurisprudential gifts granted Justices Souter, Kennedy, and O'Connor to sign their names to a text exhorting the American people to prove they possess a virtuous national character—apparently through the act of allowing their value judgments to be overridden by a panel of solemn bureaucrats mouthing the words of judicial clerks (an operation called "submitting to the rule of law.")

Nevertheless lawyers as a class are hardly insensible to the advantages of arational decision making, even within the formal confines of the courtroom itself. Observers of our litigation system are sometimes bemused by the sight of a judge at a trial's end reading two hours of extraordinarily technical and complex instructions to a jury. These directions are often barely comprehensible to the lawyers in the courtroom, and there is no reason to imagine that the jury takes away more than the most rudimentary understanding of how it is being told to go about deciding the issues at hand. This particular ritual is often cited by critics of American law as proof of our willingness to tolerate irrational, atavistic features at the heart of our dispute processing system. Yet the reading of an incomprehensible charge to the jury can be reinterpreted not as an example of irrationalism, but rather as the secret cunning of reason at work.

Condemnations of the jury system would hold more sting if there were good reasons to believe juries often decide questions that are usefully amenable to rational analysis. But, for reasons predicted by the efficient process theory, such questions rarely get before juries. The enormously high settlement rate for both criminal and civil litigation indicates not just an understandable desire to avoid transaction costs, but an acknowledgment that a conflict that is sufficiently controversial to go before a jury will as a practical matter have to be decided more or less arationally. Questions that involve significant problems of knowledge (what do we mean by "beyond a reasonable doubt"?) or that implicate deeply conflicting value systems (should individuals or society as a whole absorb the direct cost of unfortunate accidents?) can be analyzed usefully only up to a point—a distressingly modest point. Then a decision must be made. Under such conditions, the observation that asking lay juries to resolve difficult legal questions is like deciding issues by flipping coins is not nearly so devastating a criticism as the glib technocrats and secular theologians in our midst imagine it to be.

Needless to say, the American legal system doesn't always exhibit such a wholesome tendency to ignore the siren call of rationalist excess. Indeed, those texts that the legal system in general, and legal education in particular, fixate on as the very embodiments of "the law"—the mass of appellate court opinions—often resemble nothing so much as monuments to the ways in which an excessive faith in reason can come to resemble a form of mental illness. Legal scholars as ideologically diverse as Robert Nagel, Daniel Farber, and Morton Horowitz have pointed out various ways in which contemporary legal writing has come to manifest the worst forms of bureaucratic obsessionalism. Here is Horowitz's evaluation of a year's worth of recent Supreme Court opinions:

> With three or four "prong" tests everywhere and for everything; with an almost medieval earnestness about classification and categorization; with a theological attachment to the determinate power of various "levels of scrutiny"; with amazingly fine distinctions that produce multiple opinions, designated in Parts, sub-parts, and sub-sub-parts, this is a Court whose Justices appear caught in the throes of various methodological obsessions.

Yet this sort of critique, accurate as it is, can hardly be limited to judicial texts. No better demonstration of the more general point can be found than in that exemplar of the American legal mind gone off the rails, the body of materials called "constitutional theory." Examine any litigated issue in this area and you will find essentially the same situation. Among legal academics, everyone from the most self-consciously critical thinkers to the most traditionally minded doctrinalists produces contributions to the literature that track the same basic interpretive structure:

1. The extant law of _____ (the establishment clause, the free exercise clause, freedom of speech, takings, criminal procedure, the death penalty, equal protection, etc., etc.,) is an incoherent mess, made up of conclusory and muddled doctrines embodied in methodologically

useless multifactor tests that decide nothing and that no one even pretends to take seriously.

2. All previous attempts to derive a coherent and workable theory from this material have failed miserably. Therefore,

3. Here's mine.

Constitutional law theory thus mimics the implicit rhetorical structure of the standard constitutional law opinion, i.e., "Where all others before me have failed to bring forth light from darkness, I (the judge, the scholar) will exert my singular cognitive abilities and/or exemplary moral character to part the mists of ignorance and confusion that envelop this issue and thereby reveal What the Constitution Requires." It says something about the hold rationalism exerts over America's legal and cultural imagination that the absurdity of such claims is not more self-evident.

In fact the efficient process theory predicts that, given the structure of our legal system, any area of social conflict that is categorized under the rubric "constitutional law" will be a theoretical disaster area. In the American legal system, to call something a question of constitutional law is not so much an act of formal categorization as it is a shorthand way of signaling that it involves the most intractable moral and political issues our society faces. Constitutional law is the categorical dumping ground for everything the normal political process can't digest: race and religion, sex and death. All the things one should never bring up in polite conversation. *Of course* it is incoherent: you were thinking that perhaps we lawyers were going to *solve* some of these problems?

Indeed, nothing in the rich and variegated history of Anglo-American law is more ridiculous than when a court takes it on itself to announce its solution to this or that tragic conflict of politics, culture, or life. The most extreme example in this genre, setting a standard that will be difficult to surpass, is that moment in the *Casey* opinion where three Supreme Court justices cast their gaze on the enormous political and moral controversy surrounding the legality of abortion—a controversy inflamed, if not actually created, by

previous judicial pronouncements on the same subject—and proceed to "call [on] the contending sides of a national controversy to
end their national division by accepting a common mandate rooted
in the Constitution." Why, we might wonder, don't they just issue a
writ of mandamus against unwanted pregnancies or, better still,
grant a preliminary injunction against bad consequences of any
kind? Here we see how in its decadence hypertrophied rationality
mutates into something that becomes difficult to distinguish from
frank irrationalism.

The efficient process theory predicts that random, unpredictable
decisions are exactly what we should expect to find as we approach
the terminal point in an efficient dispute processing system. The
American legal process fulfills this prediction in a healthy way when
it adopts, explicitly or implicitly, arational mechanisms for deciding
rationally undecidable disputes. It illustrates the theory in a pathological fashion when it expends enormous amounts of time and
money producing texts—appellate court opinions—that in fact
follow, as any experienced attorney will admit, random, arational
patterns of outcome, and yet claim to answer the legal questions
presented by such disputes in rationally dispositive and hence predictable ways.

Note that if the theory is correct, a dispute processing system that
engages routinely in an elaborate rational analysis of disputes that
have approached the system's terminal point *must* contain significant
elements of dysfunctional reasoning. For either the disputants are
failing to perceive or choosing to ignore what that analysis requires
(in which case the system is inefficient), or the decision makers are
deceiving themselves when they assume such an analysis is in fact
possible (in which case arational decisions are being reached
through an irrational process of elaborate rationalization). I have
suggested that, on the whole, the American legal system is an efficient dispute processing mechanism, and that the hypertrophied
reasoning found in appellate court opinions is evidence of the rationalist delusions of judges and their academic imitators, rather
than of widespread craziness or stupidity on the part of litigants and

their lawyers. But this is only a suggestion: readers can decide for themselves.

A Necessary Madness?

To this point, my account has ignored what seems a pragmatic contradiction: if most actual or potential legal disputes in our society are processed employing roughly appropriate levels of rational analysis, why then are those disputes that lawyers and, especially, legal academics think of as "the law" subjected to such dysfunctional and indeed frankly irrational levels of rationalist inquiry? Why do certain disputes that could have been resolved in weeks instead drag on for years? And why do courts write 200-page opinions analyzing matters that are in fact not amenable to further analysis? I believe answering these questions requires we examine what in the American legal system are three major impediments to rational dispute processing: overgeneralization regarding the powers of rational analysis, professional vanity, and fear.

One of the peculiarities of the modern world is a certain axiomatic assumption made—often unconsciously—by many avowedly secular intellectuals. The assumption is that human reason is sufficient unto whatever tasks it should set for itself. What is peculiar about this is that without some kind of teleological account, which by definition remains unavailable to the secular intellectual, as to *why* human reason should have such powers, the assumption itself seems quite irrational. After all, as John Searle points out, it is simply impossible that a dog will ever understand quantum mechanics. Why are we not each of us that dog for the purposes of other forms —perhaps most forms—of knowledge? It may be that we need to adopt a heuristic fiction that assumes we can discover what we want to know; but, often enough, it *will* be a fiction.

Consider the use of reason by investors and gamblers. Is reason a powerful tool in these contexts? It is an immensely powerful tool— up to a point. Yet it is this very power that tends to lead us toward an unwarranted generalization that reason "works," when in fact the proper work of reason in such a context is to rapidly make further reasoning unreasonable. When betting on the 1997 Super Bowl, it would have been demonstrably unreasonable to wager on New England if the Patriots were only a 7-point underdog. It would have been equally unreasonable to bet on Green Bay if the Packers had been favored by 21 points. Reason certainly "works" in these (hypothetical) contexts. But when the question almost immediately became whether Green Bay should be made a 13^1/$_2$ or a 14-point favorite, rational inquiry had nothing useful left to say. Similarly, if the stock market were to offer investors a choice of buying either ten shares of Microsoft or Chrysler for a total price of $100, they would know immediately which stock to choose. But of course no financial market is going to offer investors such a choice.

The mistaken generalization to which we are all prone is to think that because employing sophisticated reasoning schemes makes sense within a particular social context, it will continue to make sense to employ those schemes as that very process of reasoning causes the analytic context to shift. In almost all social contexts, attempting to determine through the exercise of reason what the law requires makes good sense. Understandably, we want to believe it makes sense "all the way up" through the formal dispute processing system. We will especially want to believe this given that, generally, the further a dispute travels through the system, the more contentious and painful the social conflict it involves will be. But this is a rationalist myth, born of our tendency to overgeneralize about the powers of reason.

On the day they are published, lawyers study appellate court opinions in much the same way investors pore over the stock tables or gamblers watch the game highlights. If the lawyers have won they will congratulate themselves on their powers of insight; if they have lost they may rail at what they see as bad luck or the stupidity or even corruption of the decision makers. Yet in most instances the losing lawyers will eventually come to blame themselves for failing to see before the fact what seems so obvious now. After all, no one wants to believe he is wasting his time attempting to predict the unpredictable: better to see yourself as failing at your task than to confront the possible absurdity of your situation. And besides, *after the fact* there is new information to analyze: information that is usefully amenable to the application of sophisticated reasoning techniques. The outcome of the game, or the news of the merger, or the opinion in the case all have plenty of relevance to future analysis. This information will help determine the content of the next price, or the next line, or the next advice to the client.

In the actual practice of law new appellate court opinions redefine equilibrium zones, making some claims now "obviously" right or wrong, and creating fresh areas of ambiguity in the process. (Whether any particular opinion decreases, expands, or merely shifts the boundaries of a legal equilibrium zone will always be a complex and highly contextual question.) It is easy enough to overgeneralize, and hence to confuse the useful and indeed essential process of incorporating new information into future analyses with the possibility of undertaking a rational analysis of what the law will supposedly require in the context of the next appellate dispute.

To say that law works beautifully as long as people don't ask too much of it sounds suspiciously akin to claiming that medicine does wonders for those patients who are on the whole healthy. (Which, of course, is true.) Such a claim injures the professional vanity of lawyers who, naturally, want to believe they are in possession of unique skills and esoteric sources of knowledge that allow them to go beyond the relatively modest tasks of specialized bureaucrats who help maintain a smoothly running system of social coordination and dispute processing. No one, after all, works up much ideological fervor defending "the rule of accounting," or goes about claiming that generally accepted accounting standards are crucial to protecting democratic values and the American way of life. Atticus Finch was not a CPA.

The ideology of American law thus encourages lawyers to imagine themselves as masterful technocrats or freelance philosophers, purveying "rational policy solutions" or "practical wisdom" to the culture as a whole. The immensely useful work lawyers perform in maintaining the submerged portion of the island of law fails to flatter these more exalted visions of the professional self. These visions are further fueled by the legitimation needs of law schools, who must justify their place in the American university system, and therefore must claim to be producing and elaborating on a distinct body of valuable knowledge.

I know an academic, technically a professor of law, whose friends all realize can be driven to amusing fits of exasperation by the simple tactic of asking him a question concerning the substantive content of law. "Look it up in the phone book!" he exclaims, waving his arms about, if you should ever inquire into his views on how any legal dispute, real or hypothetical, will or ought to be resolved. By the "phone book" he means the conventional materials of legal analysis. And in fact most legal questions can be answered that way. As the saying goes, it isn't exactly rocket science. (A side point: my brother, who actually *is* a rocket scientist, assures me that what he does isn't, either). Anyway, legal academics fixate on those disputes whose solution can't be looked up in the phone book, in part because any enterprise that could actually provide such solutions would have to be in possession of the sort of powerful theories and effective methodologies we associate with legitimate intellectual disciplines. This in turn leads to that peculiar ritual of American legal pedagogy —the case method—in which students study various operations that managed to kill the patient so as to better describe how each was really a success.

In the end, overgeneralizations concerning the power of reason and intellectual pretensions born of professional vanity are each symptoms of fear. It is difficult for both lawyers and ordinary citizens to accept that all we can really say when faced with some intractable legal, moral, and political controversy is that it's a tough issue. Academics in particular find this unacceptable. For members of the professional intelligentsia this is the equivalent of being a mechanic who, after peering under a dank and odiferous hood, can only turn to the stranded driver and announce that the car's engine isn't working. Hence the compulsive solution-mongering of American academics, especially legal academics, who rarely feel they are doing their job at all unless they are purporting to solve some basic conflict of social life.

America has never been a fatalistic culture, except to the extent we have always believed it our manifest destiny to be "progressing" toward something or the other. Faced with the prospect of existential dread at our helplessness before the mysteries of life, we look for someone or something that can dispel that uncanny sensation. Hence, despite our vaunted pragmatism, we are prone to a certain child-like faith that some person or institution will with a single heroic gesture free us from the intolerable webs of uncertainty surrounding our most difficult choices. In the American law school, the most striking evidence of this faith is the way in which an entire generation of legal academics almost literally worships the Warren Court. The continuing fascination that long-departed institution holds for law professors of a certain age resembles in some ways a collective case of arrested emotional development. The kindly image of Earl Warren himself, with his grandfatherly shock of white hair, and his famed willingness to brush aside legal technicalities with the question "But is it right, is it fair?" helps satisfy the longing for some paternal figure in comforting ceremonial garb—a sort of juridical Santa Claus—who goes about dispensing justice in much the same way reformed misers in Dickens shower pounds and guineas on everyone they meet.

It may be that an explanation as to why, in the course of deciding certain elaborate legal conflicts, an otherwise fairly rational system of social coordination and dispute processing indulges in such excesses of hypertrophied reasoning can be found by distinguishing between what we ask of the visible and the invisible portions of the legal system. Someone once remarked that a serious gambler doesn't gamble to win money—he wins money in order to gamble. Perhaps we look to the visible law not so much for answers to the unanswerable, but to submit ourselves to the will of those who assure us they have such answers. Joseph de Maistre, the great enemy of rationalist, social contractarian visions of law understood this. Isaiah Berlin sums up Maistre's view of the matter:

> Men—moral beings—must submit freely to authority: but they must submit. . . . No man, and no society, can govern itself; such an expres-

sion is meaningless: all government comes from some unquestioned coercive authority. Lawlessness can only be stopped by something from which there is no appeal. It may be custom, or conscience, or a papal tiara, or a dagger, but it is always a *something*.

The invisible law—that submerged island that helps determine the shape and texture of our ordinary social lives—has no need for such obscure justifications. Here, the modest work of day-to-day cooperation can take place without recourse to that mystical something from which there is no appeal. But for the deepest questions and conflicts, the modesty of a law made present to us through its absence won't do.

For Maistre, nothing was more absurd than the naive enlightenment faith that society could be held together by factors as humble as reciprocal self-interest and neighborly forbearance: "What this religion [of the state and its laws] demands is not conditional obedience—the commercial contract of Locke ... but the dissolution of the individual in the state. ... Society is not a bank, a limited liability company formed by individuals who look on each other with suspicious eyes." The visible law, which must choose—and, if the efficient process theory is correct, choose *arbitrarily*—between the deepest commitments, the dearest values those who are subject to its will struggle to cherish and defend, must be made of sterner stuff.

The hypertrophied rationalism of American appellate law in general, and of constitutional law in particular, can then perhaps be understood and—who knows?—even justified, as a species of necessary madness: as our own version of whatever atavistic faith must ultimately undergird the violence of the state. It is the true sovereignty of law as unreasoning and unquestionable fiat, masquerading, as it must in our hyperrational world, as the very embodiment of reason itself.

5

RATIONALIZATION AND
ITS DISCONTENTS

He who possesses strength divests himself of mind.

NIETZSCHE

Six thousand years ago, the peoples of the Nile valley began to bury their dead in ways that indicated they believed the departed would go on to an afterlife. At first, such rituals were limited to including a few household implements inside the modest burial sites within which the corpses were placed. Then followed the practice of mummification to preserve the body itself, and the gradual elaboration of the place of burial. Eventually these practices culminated in the building of enormous tombs for persons of high social rank, a practice that itself reached its apogee with the construction of the great Pyramids at Giza in the twenty-sixth century B.C. The only surviving wonders of the ancient world, they still rise out of the boundless sands of the Sahara as durable monuments to the theological obsessions of the Pharaohs, obsessions that eventually caused a huge portion of the wealth of a great civilization to be poured into the building of tombs.

"Hypertrophy" is the name given to the anthropological concept that attempts to describe and explain such extreme processes of ritualistic elaboration. Today, the American legal system is rife with examples of this phenomenon: the three-day deposition, the six-month trial, the decade-long appeal, and the various textual progeny of these rituals: the 100-page appellate court opinion, the 200-page, 500-footnote law review article, the 1,000-page statute, the 16,000-page set of administrative regulations. Such rituals and texts are examples of that hypertrophy of rationalism I have called "juridical saturation," which itself is a consequence of the belief that the best way to attack a problem is to inflict a comprehensive regulatory scheme on the social context in which the problem occurs. This belief in turn produces those vast texts the sight of which cause even the most stout-hearted attorney to quail in fear: the Internal Revenue Code, the *Congressional Record*, the administrative regulations of any government agency.

What I will explore here are some implicit ideological messages, inculcated through the process of legal education, that help contribute to hypertrophied rationalism in legal thought.

Finding the Law

In August of 1940 Duncan Hannah, a lance-corporal of the British Royal Artillery, found a brooch covered with cobwebs and dirt, which someone had lodged into one of the window frames at Gwernhaylod House, a country manor that had been requisitioned by the British Army. Two months later he informed his commanding officer of his find, who suggested he turn it over to the police. A little more than two years later the police turned the brooch over to Major Hugh Edward Ethelston Peel, who had bought Gwernhaylod House in December 1938, but who had never lived in it prior to its requisitioning ten months later. Soon after, Peel got a letter from Hannah's lawyers demanding Peel give the brooch to Hannah, whereupon Peel immediately sold the brooch to a jeweler. Hannah then sued Peel for the value of the brooch.

Hannah v. Peel has become a classic case in the study of modern Anglo-American property law. Law students who are required to grapple with it are confronted with a maze of conflicting formal rules, instrumental concerns, and ethical norms. The opinion in the case is the work of a certain Judge Birkett, who at first glance comes across from the text of his opinion as a well-meaning sort, totally out of his depth when trying to negotiate his way through this particular jurisprudential labyrinth. Indeed, Birkett's opinion has become something of a pedagogical byword for how not to go about the analysis of legal issues. (In fact Judge Birkett was a very distinguished attorney: among his many accomplishments he was by general consensus the best English criminal defense lawyer of his time; and he was chosen to be one of his country's judges at the Nuremberg trials.) But of course whether or not Judge Birkett's opinion is actually a deficient example of legal reasoning depends on whether or not the case could be analyzed in some more effective manner.

Judge Birkett attempts, at least in theory, to decide the case by the common law method of deducing a rule of decision from similar past cases. This species of legal conceptualism has been famously criticized for being an elaborate form of question-begging, and I will not belabor those criticisms here. In brief, many critics have noted that the forms of analogical reasoning lawyers and judges typically employ are always fraught with ambiguities and dangers, the most noteworthy being the inescapable problems inherent in the task of determining which similarities and differences between cases are significant and which are trivial. Thus when deciding the case in this way, Judge Birkett must attempt to fit *Hannah v. Peel* into a conceptual framework that will require he give an inevitably controversial interpretation of the legal "meaning" of several disparate disputes.

For example, in the case of *Bridges v. Hawkesworth*, a salesman found a bundle of pound notes on the floor of a shop. He gave them to the shop's owner, who held the notes in the hope that their true owner would appear and claim them. After three years, the salesman asked for the notes, but the shop's owner refused to turn them over. At the conclusion of the subsequent lawsuit the appellate court awarded them to the salesman on the grounds that, first, he was the finder of a lost item, and, second, the shop owner had never been in possession of the notes before the salesman found them.

By contrast, in *South Staffordshire Water Co. v. Sharman*, a case in which the defendant found two rings at the bottom of a pool on land owned by the plaintiff, the appellate court awarded the rings to the plaintiff, asserting that "the possession of land carries with it possession of everything which may be on or in that land." The court distinguished the *Bridges* case on the basis that in those circumstances the bank notes were found in the public part of the shop, and therefore(?) were never in the possession of the shop's owner.

After describing one other case, in which a prehistoric boat was awarded to the owner of the land in which it was buried rather than to the boat's finder, again on the grounds that the owner of the land had "possession" of the lost item, Judge Birkett notes "a review of these judgments shows that the authorities are in an unsatisfactory state." He concludes it is fairly clear that "a man possesses everything that is attached to or under his land," but that "he does not necessarily possess a thing which is lying unattached on the surface of his land even though the thing is not possessed by someone else." He also notes, correctly, that the rules governing what lost items the owner of land possesses by the mere fact that he owns the land on which they are found have "never been very clearly formulated in our law." Before turning to how Judge Birkett eventually untangled this conceptual knot, let us review the situation and consider how he might go about doing so.

In the Anglo-American legal world ownership of lost property tends to be governed by two general propositions, both of which are reflected in the disputes Judge Birkett discusses. First, it is said the finder of a lost item has a better claim to it than anyone save the item's "true" owner. Yet it is also commonly asserted that the possessor of land is entitled to all lost items found on that land. The second proposition isn't a formal exception to the first; rather, as *Bridges v. Hawkesworth* illustrates, the two rules often contradict each other.

If we consider the explicit and tacit social norms these legal rules reflect, it shouldn't surprise us that the norms produce contradictory rules. As the editors of the leading property casebook for American law students suggest, among those norms might be counted the desire to get lost items back to their original owners, to carry out the respective expectations of finders and owners of land on which lost items are found, to reward both honesty and luck, and to do all these things as cheaply as possible. Note that because attempts to pursue any one of these norms will often conflict with the pursuit of some or all of the others, we can expect the legal rules that govern these situations will also tend to conflict with each other. Judge Birkett attempts to skirt any inquiry into the various conflicting instrumental purposes of finders law by framing the question conceptually: as between Corporal Hannah and Major Peel, which litigant had "prior possession" of the brooch? But the legal concept of possession is of course an artifact of legal reasoning itself, which is to say it is a socially constructed concept rather than a plain fact of nature; thus if this concept is constructed in a sufficiently ambiguous manner to allow either party to be "in" possession, the formal invocation of the concept will only beg the question. And, in a legal culture whose norms properly mirror the norms of the broader culture from which law springs, we can predict the concept *will* be sufficiently ambiguous to accommodate the essential tensions between the various social values the legal concept reflects. Let us consider some of those tensions.

The following instrumental paradox will beset any social coordination mechanism trying to produce a general rule that aims at returning lost items to their owners: if finders have a legal right to keep what they find, then the items they find will soon be untraceable by their original owners (because finders will themselves become subsequently hard to find). Yet if finders are not given rights over their finds, then we can suppose they will tend not to come forward at all. If, by contrast, we could be reasonably certain that awarding lost items to the owners of property on which the items were found would not serve as a disincentive to honesty on the part of finders, then we could best serve the goal of returning items to their original owners by awarding the items to the owners of the sites where those items were lost (because the losers of items could then successfully retrace their steps to the site of the loss). Thus even if decision makers could be certain they were operating within the confines of a broad social consensus that returning lost items to their owners was the paramount goal of finders' law, their pursuit of that coherent goal would still involve a delicate practical judgment regarding what the likely effect of any particular incentive structure might be. It should be unnecessary to add that courts have no realistic way of gathering the sort of empirical data that would allow this judgment to be something more than a very rough guess, made up of equal parts amateur sociological speculation, basic folk psychology, and seat-of-the-pants intuition.

But as a matter of fact the social consensus that would allow legal decision makers to achieve even this level of coherent helplessness doesn't exist. The social judgment that the organizing principle of finders law is to return lost items to their original owners flies in the face of the universal dictum, "finders keepers, losers weepers." At some very crude level of cultural generalization it is simply the case that those who find lost items expect to be allowed to keep them. This expectation is recognized by the general rule that a finder's right to lost property is superior to that of everyone other than the property's true owner.

Yet the actual social context is more complicated still. Corporal Hannah had the good luck to put his hand blindly on a valuable piece of lost jewelry, and naturally enough he feels his claim to the item is a valid one. But then of course Major Peel had the good luck to buy a house with a valuable old brooch hidden in a window frame. Just as naturally, he believes the brooch should be deemed his —not because that decision will facilitate getting it back to its original owner, but because the brooch was found in *his* house, which is to say within the confines of a place that is to some degree an extension of its owner's sense of self.

As for rewarding honesty, Corporal Hannah came forward in the first place, yet his honesty in these circumstances was perhaps not as exemplary as we might wish: it did, after all, take him two months to confess the existence of the brooch to his commanding officer. At a still more general level of ethical judgment we might well want to reward a soldier serving his country in time of war. Yet Major Peel is a soldier too; and whether or not he is on active duty, he has had to sacrifice his house to the quartering of other soldiers. But then again, Major Peel has never actually lived in the house, so to what extent are his expectations of ownership bound up with this particular place? On the other hand hasn't he failed to live in it only because it was requisitioned . . . ? and so on and so on.

All this is to say that the ethical considerations in the case seem to require just as delicate a judgment as does the instrumental task of assessing what sort of relatively cross-contextual legal rule will return lost items to their original owners. And we have already seen that if we try to decide the outcome of the case conceptually—by attempting to determine which party had prior legal "possession" of the brooch—the predictably ambiguous character of the formal legal materials will force us to beg the question of just what *are* the circumstances of which legal possession consists.

Today, law students are often taught to see the circularity of such conceptual arguments; thus the leading property case book asks students if the losing party in *Hannah v. Peel* lost "because he did not have prior possession, or did he not have prior possession because he lost?" In the modern American law school, future lawyers are told—sometimes explicitly, more often implicitly—to analyze such "hard" cases in the light of something called "policy," that is, to make the analysis turn primarily on the pursuit of instrumental goals rather than on an attempt to follow pre-existing legal rules. In any dispute where the formal legal materials are ambiguous (i.e., in all serious appellate cases) students are usually told that legal reasoning requires they determine what sorts of legal rules will both address the various ethical concerns the case presents, and at the same time achieve whatever instrumental goal or goals the dispute processing system wishes to pursue. Furthermore, law professors who recall that time and money are scarce commodities will remind students that any attempt to answer these questions should be pursued at a reasonable cost.

It is part of the rationalist dogma underlying American legal ideology that undertaking such an analysis always makes sense; hence the criticism heaped on Judge Birkett for failing to do so in the course of deciding *Hannah v. Peel*. But the task of making difficult legal questions usefully amenable to rational analysis faces many obstacles.

Consider as an initial matter the question of whether conflicts between finders and property owners should be resolved by reference to so-called "bright line" rules or to more amorphous legal standards. In one sense almost all jurisprudential arguments can be reduced to some variation of this classic, irresolvable debate. The debate is irresolvable because the strengths of each approach will always magnify the weaknesses of its alternative. Clear, easily applicable rules have the advantages associated with certainty and predictability and the disadvantages as well: the general efficiency of such rules always comes at the cost of injustice in the odd particular case. All rules by their nature *as* rules must be both over-and under-inclusive in regard to the behavior they are intended to regulate: as Aristotle noted at that historical moment halfway between the building of the pyramids and our own time, to decide by reference to rule is to forego the relative accuracy of case-by-case judgment. By contrast, fuzzy legal standards allow for particularistic, context-sensitive judgments that are by *their* nature prone to all the high processing costs and subjective arbitrariness such judgments inevitably produce.

Thus a case such as *Hannah v. Peel* might be decided by reference to a hard-edged rule ("lost objects go to those who find them"; "lost items found in or on private property go to the owner of the property") or a fuzzy legal standard ("lost objects go to whatever party has the most reasonable expectations of ownership"). The respective rules are fairly easy to apply, yet that very ease of application guarantees that from time to time the results of their application will seem blatantly unfair. The proffered standard sounds good, but it has the disadvantage of not allowing parties to predict very readily how their dispute will be resolved; and it also gives decision makers no real guidance, beyond telling them to do what seems best in the course of sorting out the endlessly protean circumstances of particular legal disputes.

In any decisional context where various important social norms are in tension, the dispute processing system will tend to produce either seemingly clear rules that to some extent contradict each other, and therefore don't really resolve difficult intermediate cases, or fuzzy standards that hardly even pretend to do so. Often a synthetic approach develops in which apparently rigid rules are modified by vague, standard-like exceptions. Historically this latter pattern was formalized in the common law system by the division of courts into those of "law" and "equity," with the former aspiring to the domain of the certain, and the latter to the honorific of the just. Indeed it is likely that, given the respective strengths and weaknesses of rules and standards, all developed legal cultures will to a certain degree oscilate between them. Some dialectical pattern, whereby a seemingly certain rule is eroded by the gradual accretion of standard-like exceptions to its application, until the increasing amorphousness of the exceptions produces a rule-like counter-reaction, is probably an inevitable feature of any elaborate dispute processing system.

What Judge Birkett thinks of as "the law" that governs *Hannah v. Peel* seems to be a law of rules: lost property belongs to the finder, and lost items in or on private property go to the owner of that property. Yet if either of these apparently clear rules is enforced with any consistency across various unforseeable social contexts, what will be felt to be obviously inequitable results are sure to follow. Instead of simply tolerating the costs of such results the dispute processing system interprets the two rules so that they contradict rather than complement each other; thus, in cases such as this one, the invocation of the rules can by itself decide nothing.

All of this is, as I say, exceedingly well known. What isn't sufficiently appreciated are the ultimate implications of such insights for the practice of legal reasoning.

Hannah v. Peel is yet another example of a dispute that takes place in a social and legal equilibrium zone. Again, a social equilibrium zone is an area of moral and political judgment in which various powerful, widely held, and rationally irrefutable beliefs—beliefs not amenable to either rational confirmation or rebuttal—can be adduced for holding contradictory positions regarding controversial issues. A legal equilibrium zone develops whenever the materials of legal interpretation faithfully reflect this underlying cultural tension, by failing to resolve through formal rules social conflicts that are not otherwise usefully amenable to rational analysis. When faced with such conflicts legal thinkers have three options: they can deny the failure of formal legal reasoning; they can admit this failure and yet deny the failure of reason more broadly conceived; or they can acknowledge their true situation. In the American law school members of the first group are called "formalists," while those of the second are usually identified as "realists" or, in their more overtly politicized modes, "critical legal thinkers." As for the third group it either never existed at all or has been hunted to the verge of extinction. (We will have to abandon the trim turf of the academic suburbs for the wilds of actual legal practice to find representatives of this latter species.)

The eternally recurring conflict between rules and standards is just one example of the rational wheel-spinning that takes place whenever decision makers attempt to analyze conflicts within a legal equilibrium zone. Yet many other problems beset the more explicitly instrumental forms of analysis recommended by up-to-date legal thinkers, who believe they hold formalism in contempt and hence insist that "we are all realists now." Let us consider three.

First, and most obvious, how will we choose what instrumental goal to pursue? It is all very well to scoff at formalism in favor of result-oriented legal reasoning, but just how is this "reasoning" going to take place? As Richard Posner points out in the course of discussing Alasdair MacIntyre's book-length demonstration of the same point, "There is no rational way of resolving [controversial moral issues] in a society as morally diverse as ours." (Posner is speaking specifically of abortion, but MacIntyre's argument applies to all significant moral controversies.) The standard reply that we can still reason about such matters is quite beside the point. After all, we can, and often do, undertake impossible interpretive activities; yet our willingness to do so doesn't make the interpretations that result from those activities any more compelling to those who disagree with our conclusions—nor indeed should it.

Note this recognition of the problem of moral indeterminacy isn't a product of a pragmatically trivial skepticism that asserts we can never actually be "certain" of anything. The real problem is much deeper. It isn't merely that we can't be *certain* our beliefs about deeply controversial moral issues are in fact true; rather, the real difficulty is that under current cultural conditions we cannot give *any* recognizably valid reasons why those who disagree with us about such issues should change their minds.

Within such a culture impassioned moral and political debate will tend to devolve into the bald assertion of intuitive belief masquerading as rationally compelling argument. For example, let us suppose Dick thinks that affirmative action is a moral imperative, while Jane considers it an ethical abomination. If they are professors of moral philosophy, we can be fairly certain they will proceed to insist that their respective political commitments are impelled by something they call "reason." If they are elite lawyers—and especially if they are judges or legal academics—we may surmise they will identify those commitments with "what the Constitution requires (or forbids)." God knows they wouldn't do this if they were arguing about the relative merits of Häagen-Dazs and Ben & Jerry's.

My point here isn't that moral beliefs are merely subjective and therefore nothing more than manifestations of arational preference, but rather that, in a society that doesn't feature enough widely held axiomatic moral agreement on fundamental ethical questions, there simply isn't any way of distinguishing between subjective or intersubjective preference and objective moral truth. (The supposed postmodern "insight" that these things are actually identical attempts to eliminate this interpretive crisis by enshrining it.)

Second, as I noted earlier, even if they should happen to agree on what instrumental goals the law ought to pursue, legal decision makers generally lack access to both the initial information and the sorts of informational feedback structures that would allow them to predict with confidence what the effects of a particular decisional outcome are likely to be. This is not, of course, a problem unique to law, although it is one to which—perhaps by necessity—the legal form of thought remains particularly oblivious. By contrast, contemporary natural and social science has shown in rich detail how almost any systemic action will cause a myriad of unforeseen, and indeed unforseeable, reactions. Thus biologists have traced how the disappearance of an obscure parasite can bring about the collapse of an entire ecosystem, while sociologists have demonstrated how even the most careful, empirically informed attempts to affect social structures often have more powerful unintended than intended consequences, with the effects of the former perversely overwhelming any benefits gained from the latter.

The recent history of American law is full of such examples. We have seen how the liberal legal scholar's insistence on continually elaborating the due process rights of the accused has ended in the functional elimination of the constitutional right to a trial for all but a tiny percentage of criminal defendants: our legal system has found it simply impossible, as a practical matter, to actually carry out those generous procedures.* Ironically it has been through the exploitation of public anger and resentment, generated by the supposed effects of these well-publicized yet mostly illusory "rights," that conservative politicians have managed to bring about a fourfold per capita increase in the U.S. prison population over the past twenty-five years. These radical, symbiotic shifts in social policy have happened without the aid of any systematic institutional or budgetary planning, and (as we will see in the particular context of the so-called "war on drugs") they have together combined to produce extremely dubious social effects.

Along similar lines, consider how more than a generation after the Supreme Court declared school segregation unconstitutional, America's urban school systems are now more segregated than they were the day that brave, hubristic declaration was uttered: an outcome that in some respects was a product of unanticipated social consequences resulting from the declaration itself. Indeed, the political scientist Gerald Rosenberg's recent book *The Hollow Hope* illustrates in powerful detail how the progressive politics of judicial review have often backfired in just this fashion. For instance, the practice of liberal judicial review has played an unforeseen yet cru-

---

*In Colorado in 1995, 96 percent of all criminal convictions were obtained without the benefit of a trial.

cial role in producing that unified and politically influential social and political movement often called "the religious right"—a political movement that depends for its strength on various intense public controversies, that in turn owe much of *their* intensity, and even their very existence, to controversial judicial decisions on matters such as abortion, busing, the rights of criminal defendants, and school prayer.

If we descend to the level of farce, we have the recent example of the Supreme Court of New Jersey's attempt to protect lawyers from an upsurge in legal malpractice suits. That court interpreted a statute of limitations in a highly restrictive manner, thereby effectively barring a large subclass of such suits unless those suits were filed very soon after litigants who switched lawyers in the course of ongoing cases obtained new representation. What was supposed to be a prophylactic interpretation, designed to forestall malpractice suits, instead caused a sevenfold increase in legal malpractice actions—because newly hired lawyers were afraid *they* would be liable for malpractice if they failed to inform their new clients that they had to sue their former lawyers immediately or forever hold their peace.

A particularly compelling series of narratives, illustrating the perverse instrumental effects legal rules often have, is found in Thomas Geoghegan's wonderfully funny and sad indictment of American labor law, *Which Side Are You On?* Rules intended originally to protect the rights of workers to organize and join unions have become so bureaucratized, so complex, and so contradictory that they often make it feasible for those with the requisite resources (i.e., management) to manipulate the legal interpretation of these rules so as to make effective unionization all but impossible. Here is part of his account of an attempt to organize a small group of nurses in rural Illinois, under what should have been ideal conditions for unionization (a shortage of qualified workers, bad employment conditions, etc.). Capturing the thickly descriptive quality of Geoghegan's almost anthropological picture of the madness of American labor law requires an extended quotation:

But organizing [the nurses] is a nightmare. I know of [National Labor Relations] Board cases pending for *seven* years. Think of it: Seven years ago, a union asked a group of nurses to sign cards, risk their jobs, and said at the time, perhaps, "Look, this'll go fast." Now, seven years later, the Board and the court are still trying to decide whether one little clutch of nurses should be in a union together—whether they are, in a legal sense, "an appropriate bargaining unit." What, you say, is an "appropriate bargaining unit?" . . . There are hundreds, maybe thousands [of possible employee permutations] and a good management lawyer will raise each one. Not just raise it, but brief it, put on witnesses, ask for a ruling, and then do it all again for another permutation. And I, the Union lawyer, have to argue it, brief it, as if we were talking about something serious. . . .

Meanwhile, the hospital is firing all the nurses it can.

And meanwhile, the Board is changing the rules for deciding what is "an appropriate bargaining unit." Since the cases drag on for years, the rules can change two or three times in the course of one case. A few years ago, the Board tried to codify the rules in a decision known as *St. Francis Hospital*, or *St. Francis I*. Then it came up with new rules in *St. Francis II*. Since a federal judge has just thrown out *St. Francis II*, we are all now waiting for *St. Francis III*. And after *St. Francis III*, there will be a puff of white smoke, and we will have *St. Francis IV*, and then *St. Francis V*, in dynastic succession, like a long line of popes. One day, when I am old, and young lawyers are at my knee and asking me about *St Francis XXIII*, maybe I will shock them by saying, "I remember *St. Francis I*."

Meanwhile, the nurses wait and wait, their hair turns white. If a nurse is fired, I say to her, "You're going to file a charge, I hope."

"Where?" she says.

"The NLRB."

"THERE? *That* place?"

"Well, where did you think?"

"How long is this going to take?"

"Three years."

She looks at me as if I'm nuts. I don't even tell her the truth, which is that for three years she'll see her name dragged through the mud, with doctors, administrators, even parking lot attendants coming in to say:

"She didn't change the patient's bedpan."

"I saw her yelling at a patient."

"I saw her flirting with a patient."

"I saw her having *sex* with a patient."

And finally: "She's on drugs."

And the hospital can swing away, since in a hearing it has absolute protection from libel.

Sure she should file a charge. Kafka would file a charge.

This is the hypertrophy of the urge to regulate. This is what happens when a legal system forgets that the more it elaborates itself, the more manipulable the system will become, and the more unpredictable the social effects of such manipulation will be. In the face of thousands of such sobering examples the modern instrumental vision of law as "policy science" remains little more than a series of hopeful guesses, a pseudo-science conducted with much bravado but little real data and no valid method of experimentation; and, despite the shallow technocratic optimism of its rhetoric it remains hard to see how, as a practical matter, it could ever be anything more.

Third, instrumental visions of law are all more or less dependent on the assumption that people "know" what the law is. But, especially at the level of technical specificity at which people would have to know the law for much instrumental legal reasoning to make sense, this assumption is almost always a blatant fiction.

George Fletcher has made the amusing observation that one of the few technical rules of criminal law the lay public actually knows is that ignorance of it is no excuse. Consider in this light the classic instrumental analysis of finders problems. This analysis turns on how to mediate tensions in the incentive structures supposedly created by rules that either reward or penalize finders for coming forward with lost property. Now of course the saliency of such an analysis must hinge on finders knowing what those rules are. But finders almost literally *never* know the rules, which in any case are often so ambiguous and contradictory that "knowing" them would be of little practical use. With the exception of those few people who engage routinely in searches for lost or abandoned property (salvage operations, etc.) almost all lost property is found by persons who are perfectly ignorant of the governing rules, and who therefore remain immune to any instrumental incentives the rules might be thought to promote.

Every year I teach *Hannah v. Peel* to my Property class of first-year law students. I always conclude a complicated instrumental analysis of finders law by asking students how many of them knew the most general rules of that law (i.e., lost property generally goes to the finder, but locus owners have strong claims) before they studied this case. The answer, invariably, is "none." This fact is all the more sobering if we consider these students are all part of a highly educated subgroup of the populace that has an unusual interest in legal questions. My informal surveys only reflect what more sophisticated studies have demonstrated: the general public almost never knows the content of the law at a level of specificity that would allow even the crude instrumental calculations of judges—let alone the subtler analyses of academics—to affect social behavior in any very predictable way.

Expecting to Fly

The successful rational analysis of legal questions must be based on interpretive agreement concerning either the formal concepts in question, or the instrumental goals those concepts are supposed to advance. In the latter case, further requirements of rational success are that the analysis have a sufficient empirical basis in the data and methodologies available to decision makers, and that there is a reasonable probability a decision will affect in some sufficiently predictable manner the subsequent calculations of those subject to it. We have seen how in a dispute such as that underlying the decision in *Hannah v. Peel*, none of the conditions enabling successful rational analysis is present. By definition, this will always be the case for disputes that take place inside legal equilibrium zones. As I argued in the previous chapter, almost all nonfrivolous appellate court cases are litigated within what are both broadly social and narrowly legal equilibrium zones; hence such cases are fraught with all the analytic ambiguity those zones produce. I now consider within the context of this particular case the general consequences for legal reasoning that follow from the pervasive presence of such decisional ambiguities.

As we saw, after describing the facts and the law of several previous cases Judge Birkett concludes (correctly) that "a review of these judgments shows that the authorities are in an unsatisfactory state." *Hannah v. Peel* occupies a legal equilibrium zone between a formal rule that would certainly grant the brooch to Corporal Hannah if he had found it lying on public sidewalk, and another that would almost as surely award it to Major Peel if it had been dug up out of the garden of Gwernhaylod House. (Note how this dispute takes place within a legal equilibrium zone even though it is, in terms of formal legal action, a remarkably straightforward case, featuring none of the significant factual or procedural uncertainty decision makers almost always confront when dealing with the typical litigated conflict.)

Faced with this conceptual equilibrium, Judge Birkett disdains launching on a vain search for an instrumentally desirable result, and instead merely notes that Hannah's conduct in coming forward was commendable and meritorious, and that Peel was never physically in possession of the premises. For a moment the judge seems poised to decide the matter on the specious conceptual ground that "the brooch was never [Peel's], in the ordinary acceptation of the term, in that he had the prior possession." What the ordinary meaning of the claim a property owner "possesses" an object lost on his land might be, and whether or not that meaning, once determined, should be a requirement for overcoming the finder's claims are, of course, just the questions at issue; but in the end Judge Birkett refuses to rely on such circular reasoning.

> A discussion of the merits does not seem to help, but it is clear on the facts that the brooch was "lost" in the ordinary meaning of that word, that it was "found" by the plaintiff in the ordinary meaning of that word, that its true owner has never been found, that the defendant was the owner of the premises and had his notice drawn to this matter by the plaintiff, who found the brooch. In those circumstances I propose to follow the decision in Bridges v. Hawkesworth, and to give judgment in this case for the plaintiff for £66.

What are we to make of what the editors of my students' casebook characterize as "the judge's rather remarkable statement" that "a discussion of the merits does not seem to help"? Certainly Judge Birkett avoids any such discussion; hence the almost universal academic criticism of his opinion as analytically deficient. But as a matter of fact a discussion of the merits does *not* seem to help. We have already seen that the case is conceptually indeterminate; that strong ethical claims can be made for each party; and that the question of what a sound instrumental approach to the issue would entail is both practically and theoretically intractable. Again, we can always *discuss* the merits, just as we can always "reason" about essentially contested moral and political issues. Go right ahead, if it makes you feel any better.

It remains one of the abiding vices of rationalism, especially in its various academic incarnations, that it assumes reasoning about difficult questions is always reasonable. But on those occasions when further reasoning doesn't seem to help, and yet we nevertheless continue to indulge in it anyway, what is called "reason" soon turns into something that can be positively unhelpful: an elaborate form of rationalization. Indeed, to call this activity "reasoning" brings to mind a strange young man I knew in college, who kept insisting he could fly. When challenged to prove it he would sprint down the hall of the dormitory, flapping his arms with manic glee, and shouting, "Fly! Fly! Fly!" He would then leap approximately ten feet through the air before crashing into the cinder blocks at the end of the hall. The brood of mockers in our midst—those skeptics who, always and everywhere, endeavor to ruin the sacred truths to which the faithful cling—refused to accept this evidence as definitive. Yet soon enough his version of flight became a staple of sophomoric drunkenness at the end of dorm parties, as well as a part of the ritualistic celebration of the school's athletic triumphs. At the height of the Dionysian frenzy that marked the end of semester finals (by which time, alas, our hero had been expelled for failing to attend a single class) even some of the skeptics were attempting to fly.

Judge Birkett refuses to take flight. By having the strength of mind *not to give reasons* he reminds us of how, when the weapons of reason fail, an arational, gnostic utterance can be the very mark of reason itself. The apparent *aporia* in which his argument leaves us is, perhaps, but a form of Socratic motley, whose obscuring mantle hides from us the deeper wisdom of the self-knowing fool.

Naturally, the insight that "a discussion of the merits does not seem to help" will be as disturbing to the intelligentsia as the realization that there are situations in which physical courage is of no use will be to the initiates of a warrior caste. Even as heterodox a legal thinker as Richard Posner can embrace this possibility only with considerable ambivalence. Consider an opinion written early in his judicial career, *O'Shea v. Riverway Towing*, in which Judge Posner grappled with the issue of whether a trial judge's award of damages for lost future earnings was unreasonably high. In the course of doing so he admonished the trial judge that "[u]nlike many other damage items in a personal injury case, notably pain and suffering, the calculation of damages for lost earnings can and should be an analytical rather than an intuitive undertaking." Note this is said in a decisional context that features such a profound level of analytic uncertainty (regarding how to determine, among other things, future wage rates, the probable pre-accident length of the plaintiff's career, the likely effects of inflation on both wages and financial instruments, and the best methodology, given these and other variables, for discounting to present value a hypothesized stream of future earnings—all controversial questions among professional economists) that the plaintiff's expert economist could only give a range of estimates between $50,000 and $114,000 regarding the question of what his client's lost earnings were likely to have been.

Judge Posner, of course, is well aware of the enormous empirical and theoretical difficulties any such calculation must face, even going so far as to note that "the exactness which economic analysis rigorously pursued appears to offer is, at least in the litigation setting, somewhat delusive." After an extremely learned and abstruse discussion of the different routes one might follow in making such calculations, he upholds as reasonable the district judge's award of damages, which is near the midpoint of the expert's series of estimates. Yet at the conclusion of his opinion Judge Posner takes the somewhat unusual step of chiding the lower court judge for failing to "set out the steps by which he arrived at his award for lost future earnings, in order to assist the appellate court in reviewing the award," and he asks that in the future the district judges of the circuit not neglect to do so.

Two things seem curious about this request. First, in the great majority of similar cases the award of lost future earnings will be made by a jury, who of course will provide the appellate court with no assistance regarding the question of how they came to make a particular determination. Why, we might ask, should the occasional bench trial be treated differently? Second, what practical difference does it make whether a lower court judge explains or fails to explain the purported basis for his or her decision, as long as that decision is somewhere within the range of what the reviewing court considers reasonable conclusions?

I believe the answers to these questions are closely linked. We can surmise that Judge Posner accepts the pragmatic truth that juries will make arational decisions regarding those questions he admits must be answered intuitively, or that can be analyzed in only weakly rational ways. Indeed, as we have seen, the jury can be understood as an implicitly arational mechanism for deciding questions that are not amenable to sophisticated rational analysis. The decisions of judges, on the other hand, are supposed to embody reasoned judgment rather than mere will or chance. But as Judge Posner's own analysis of the question demonstrates, in the case at hand the discounted present value of the plaintiff's hypothetical future earnings can only be determined—even given an optimistic belief in the powers of rational economic analysis—to fall somewhere within a wide zone of possible outcomes. Within this sort of analytic equilibrium zone it becomes quite arbitrary to declare some results reasonable and others unreasonable, or even to claim that some outcomes are more reasonable than others. Under such interpretive conditions, the demand for more reasons from decision makers amounts to an invitation for them to indulge in analytically pointless—yet ideologically potent—forms of juridical rationalization.

In *O'Shea v. Riverway Towing* the district judge had to make a choice from among what the most sophisticated rational analysis available indicated was a series of rationally indistinguishable alternatives. As in *Hannah v. Peel*, a discussion of the merits had produced a decisional situation in which a further discussion of the merits did not seem to help. It is precisely at this juncture in any dispute processing system that the hypertrophy of reason can begin: at that moment when the deployment of reason has worked to make its further deployment superfluous, and indeed unreasonable.

But it is in just such situations that various influential ideologies of American legal and political thought will demand we attempt to resolve the most difficult social conflicts through yet more elaborate exertions of rationalist inquiry. Faced with an impossible task, the system reacts to the cognitive dissonance these demands generate by producing those artifacts of rationalist excess that simultaneously deny and illustrate the limitations of reason: the decade-long appeal, the 100-page appellate court opinion, the 200-page law review article, the 1,000 page statute, and so on. These sorts of legal artifacts are the fruit of futile, hypertrophied exercises in forms of argument that call themselves "reason," but that in fact must conclude with the assertion of axiomatic or circular propositions. And the excessive, jurismaniacal character of such monuments to rationalist vanity can itself be understood as the product of what is in essence a kind of obsessive-compulsive reaction to the neurotic structure of American legal thought.

The ideological function of such hypertrophied texts is to grind both their writers and readers into submission: to convince us by sheer verbal hyperbole that law can provide answers to questions that defeat the resources of politics and culture. For the uninitiated lay public, the massive bulk of the endeavor combines with the technical obscurity of its language to provide a vague assurance that, surely, these people must know what they are talking about. As for lawyers, we in one sense remain more aware than that lay public of how isn't the case; after all, we know from experience that much of the time in our roles as advocates and decision makers we are, to put it bluntly, faking it. This, ironically, is why Judge Birkett's acknowledgment that a discussion of the merits does not seem to help is so rare as to shock the sensibilities of the legal mind: this admission shocks precisely because, with some part of that mind, every lawyer recognizes its truth.

It may be the case that the practice of law and, especially, the practice of judging the law—whether in the courtroom or the class-room—requires that this kind of self-knowledge remain for the most part systematically repressed. All the technocratic obfuscation and oracular resonance within which we drape our most dubious arguments may be both the law and the lawyer's way of avoiding this disturbing insight. Perhaps the legal form of life simply demands we deny the fact that, when it comes to society's most difficult issues, the makers and manipulators of law are no different from anyone else: in the end, we can't explain why we believe the things we believe or—more to the point—why those who disagree with us should be forced to act as if they believed those things as well.

The Unacknowledged Legislators

Six thousand years from now, long after the great southwestern desert has reclaimed the glittering valley the Spanish named Los Angeles, centuries after the topless towers of Manhattan have been buried under tons of geologic strata, the fecund silence of virgin forests will have once again returned to shroud the vanity and grandeur of a vanished world. What, we might wonder, will the archeology of the future make of the place its creators called "America"? If the present moment is any guide, our inconceivable descendants will pick through the remnants of a lost civilization and come to suspect that this was a people obsessed with something called "the rule of law." They will find what is left of vast temples dedicated to the cult of this god, as well as many bits of circumstan-tial evidence indicating that a great part of everyday life was given over to the scrupulous observance of its demanding rituals. They will conclude, perhaps, that the people of this nation came to believe their god could take dominion over every aspect of their lives, until an overweening pride in their deity's powers came to be inscribed on the very monuments they erected to its worship. Will there still be poets, somewhere in that undiscovered country, who will look on the ruins of what we are today? If so, may they revivify in verse the peculiar passions of a long-departed world.

I met a traveller from an antique land
Who said: Two vast and trunkless legs of stone
Stand in the desert. Near them on the sand
Half sunk, a shattered visage lies, whose frown
And wrinkled lip and sneer of cold command
Tell that its sculptor well those passions read
Which yet survive, stamped on these lifeless things,
The hand that mocked them and the heart that fed;
And on the pedestal these words appear:
"My name is Ozymandis, king of kings;
Look on my works, ye Mighty, and despair!"
Nothing beside remains. Round the decay
Of that colossal wreck, boundless and bare,
The lone and level sands stretch far away.

6

TOWARD A GENERAL THEORY
OF UNICORNS

The greatest of sorcerers would be he who could cast a spell
on himself to the degree of taking his own phantasmagoria
for autonomous apparitions. Might that not be our case?

NOVALIS, *Philological Fragments*

Once upon a time people believed that unicorns, like owls, doves,
and salamanders, lived deep in the vernal gloom of the forest.
Because unicorns were reputed to be especially clever and shy creatures, they were very difficult to find; indeed they were rarely ever
spotted except in poor light, flitting between the shadows of mossy
trees, or disappearing behind the sudden bend of a glittering stream.
Despite these impediments to their systematic study, elaborate
accounts nevertheless developed concerning their habits, appearance, and likely whereabouts. The biology and psychology of the
unicorn were subjects of immense learning; comprehensive treatises
were composed; competing theories jostled for attention; and scholars argued in heated conventicles, disputing the value of each other's
evidence, interpretations, and methods.

Then one day (or so it seemed, so sudden was the change, so
irrevocable the loss of faith) no one believed in unicorns any more.
The unicorn became a potent yet imaginary symbol; a subject of
fables and legends; an image woven into the golden threads of tapes-
tries; an emblematic herald prancing across the landscapes of
Flemish painters. No one argued about whether or not the unicorn
was really black or white or green, or whether its horn if lost in
combat actually regenerated itself. No one argued any longer that

the unicorn was "really" anything at all. Unicorns had, in one sense, ceased to exist.

But only in a sense. Are unicorns real? Of course they are: as the philosopher Max Black noted, the only appropriate answer to the question of whether or not something is real is "yes." The relevant question then becomes, "real" in what way? The story of the unicorn is the tale of a concept's migration, in the minds of men and women, from the bright sunlight of an actual forest glade into the murky realm of the fantastic. Once this journey was complete it was no longer possible to hope to find a unicorn in the forest: one had to limit that search to the precincts of poems, paintings, and dreams. Unicorns remained "real," but only in limited ways, for certain purposes. A writer could still place a unicorn amid the gilt-edged pages of a novel, but even an emperor had to dispense with the notion of actually capturing a fabulous beast that would in the cool of the evening wander the labyrinthine paths of the imperial gardens, to the wonderment of ambassadors, concubines, and saffron-robed priests.

California Is a State of Mind

Some things exist apart from us; others continue to subsist only because we think they do. The scuffed cowhide of a baseball is *there* whether people think it is or not, but the infield fly rule only comes into being when we invoke it, submit to it, exploit it, or argue about it. The state of California is at bottom a state of mind, because without such human mental states there would be no California. The cliffs of Yosemite, the bristlecone pines of the desert interior, and the mackerel-crowded seas of the southern coasts would all, of course, still be "there"; yet the state of California is not merely these things, but these things understood within the confines of a social and political concept that simply does not exist outside the belief systems created and maintained by various human minds.* If every-

---

*Whether those features of "California" that are not dependent on human cognition are themselves completely independent of *any* mind is a much more difficult

one everywhere simultaneously ingested a drug that eliminated all memory of the concept, California would at that moment be fulminated out of existence as if by some lightless fire. California is there only because, quite literally, we *think* it is there.

One of the most curious aspects of socially constructed entities is that many of them are the sorts of artifacts that can perform the social work they are supposed to accomplish only if we ignore or forget their artificial nature. A classic example of this is the socially necessary assumption that value inheres in what we call "money." As a matter of practical psychology money can function as a medium of exchange only to the extent that we manage to treat it as valuable in itself. We don't "believe" money is valuable: we *know* it is. Yet what is that knowledge other than our unconscious confidence that, in this case, knowledge and belief are not merely compatible, but actually identical? We believe we know money is valuable because we know we believe it is. In such cases, the psychology of appropriate social belief requires that we maintain an involuted state of mind in which we both know and don't know that various artifacts in whose existence we believe exist precisely because we believe they do.

Or consider in this regard the mimetic aspects of watching a film. If we keep saying to ourselves, "That's not really James Bond, those aren't real bullets," and so on, we will not maintain the appropriate mental state of belief required of the audience in the creation of the film as aesthetic experience. Yet our belief in the reality of what appears to be taking place must also be limited by our unconscious knowledge that this belief is false. We must "believe" in James Bond —but not to the extent of ducking every time he brandishes a piece of Q's devastating gadgetry.

Now films, and to a lesser extent currencies, are examples of where our knowledge of the fictional, context-specific nature of our belief remains fairly close to the surface of conscious thought. But many other psychological artifacts of contemporary life are much more cognitively complicated. To what extent do we, or should we, recognize that a concept like "the government" or "the court" is also

question than the dogmatic materialism of our culture is at present willing to acknowledge. This point will be touched on in Chapter 8.

a pragmatic and mimetic fiction? One thing is certain: given the socially constructed nature of so much of our daily experience, the structure of modern life ensures that a great deal of what we think of as "reality" will be a product of a kind of mass hypnosis, which requires that we maintain ourselves in delicately balanced, psychologically complex states of knowing ignorance and skeptical credulity. (To paraphrase Thomas Szasz: if you believe in the United States of America that's called "patriotism"; if you believe in the Republic of Texas that's called "schizophrenia.")

Which brings us to what is called "the law." In what sense does law exist? As a historical matter, it is fairly clear that at one time the lawyers and judges of the English common law thought of their law as rather more like a horse than a unicorn; that is, to the extent they considered the question at all, they believed "the law" was an objective, metaphysically robust entity. They also appeared to believe the law had existed from time immemorial and that therefore it certainly was not a product of, or dependent on, human beliefs and desires. This particular metaphysical vision—what Oliver Wendell Holmes famously called "the brooding omnipresence of the law"—cannot be maintained as a matter of self-conscious belief in a thoroughly secular, aggressively materialist public culture such as our own. In our legal culture, one can no longer assert openly the proposition that law is not an artifact of human will without running the risk of being told that anyone who could believe such a thing must be deeply confused, if not actually deluded.

Nevertheless contrary to the explicit claims of rationalizers, technocrats, and utilitarians of every stripe the implicit belief in law as a brooding omnipresence is far from dead. Indeed, given what we require of law, it may be that some degree of belief that it is "really" there—that the unicorn still inhabits some hidden hollow of the forest—remains a necessary component of the legal form of thought.

How To Do Things with Laws

In November 1968, Masako Sawada and Helen Sawada were injured when struck by a car driven by Kokichi Endo. They sued him and won judgments totaling slightly more than $25,000. During the nineteen-month period between the filing of the suits and the jury's verdicts Kokichi Endo and his wife, Ume Endo, transferred ownership of their house to their sons. The Endos continued to live in the house after the transfer, although Ume Endo died only ten days after the verdicts were returned against her husband.

The Sawadas were subsequently unable to collect their judicially decreed debt from the remaining assets of Kokichi Endo. They brought another suit, asking the court to declare the transfer of the Endo home a fraudulent conveyance, undertaken for the purpose of defrauding the property owner's creditors, and to therefore set the conveyance aside.

Ultimately, the Supreme Court of Hawaii was asked to answer the question of whether or not the manner in which the Endos had held their property precluded a finding that the transfer to their sons was fraudulent as a matter of law, no matter how "fraudulent," in ordinary lay terms, the transferors' intent may have been. The Endos had owned their house in a "tenancy by the entireties." In the English common law, property held in a tenancy by the entireties had the following relevant characteristics: it had to be owned jointly by a married couple; it could be conveyed or mortgaged by the husband, but not by the wife (at common law, a married woman was for most property-owning purposes not a juridically recognized person); it was subject to the husband's general debts; and at the death of one spouse, it was treated as if it simply remained the sole property of the surviving spouse. Thus if the husband sold or mortgaged the property and then died before his wife, the husband's interest in the estate was treated as if it had never existed, and hence the property would belong solely to his widow, unencumbered by her late husband's conveyances and debts.

With the passage of the Married Women's Property Acts in the nineteenth century, American jurisdictions removed most of the formal common law disabilities that precluded married women from controlling marital property. These statutes, however, failed to address the question of what effect they should be construed to have on the tenancy by the entireties. Various state courts subsequently answered this question in four different ways. A few states treated the tenancy as unchanged; the husband retained sole power to convey the estate, and it remained liable to his debts, subject only to the wife's right of survivorship. Other states placed the wife in what under the common law had been the husband's shoes, by making the estate liable to her separate debts as well as to his, and by allowing either spouse to sell the property. A third group placed the husband in the wife's former position, barring the separate debts of either party from affecting the estate, and not allowing either spouse to convey the estate without the consent of the other. Finally, two states allowed either spouse to subject his or her survivorship interest to creditors, but barred any separate debts from being attached to the property itself while both spouses still owned it.

By the 1970s, Hawaii remained the only state not to have addressed this particular question; and the inability of the Sawadas to collect on their debt gave the state's supreme court the opportunity to do so. For if Hawaii chose to retain the common law estate, or if it put the wife in the former position of the husband, then the Endos' transfer of their property to their sons would be treated as fraudulent as a matter of law, given that Mr. Endo's interest in the estate would still be liable to his general debts. On the other hand if Mr. Endo was placed in what under the common law was the wife's position, neither his nor his wife's separate debts could then affect the solvency of the estate, and hence as a technical matter the transfer would not be considered fraudulent.

The modern tenancy by the entireties produces some difficult conceptual puzzles. Its common law predecessor was a product of what to us seems the metaphysically mysterious idea, derived from various elements of Christian doctrine, that a husband and wife were a single legal person. This idea led to little practical difficulty as long as only one of the subjects in this consubstantial union was a juridically recognized entity. But with the legal emancipation of women, Simone de Beauvoir's observation that for the equation $1 + 1 = 1$ to work one of the integers had to, functionally speaking, become a zero could no longer adequately explain the conceptual structure of the tenancy by the entireties. As the opinion in *Sawada v. Endo* notes, "The tenancy was and still is predicated upon the legal unity of the husband and wife, but the Acts converted it into a unity of equals and not of unequals as at common law." The conceptual difficulty thus arises because under the modern view each spouse owns, in both theory and practice, the entire estate: each is deemed in the reifying jargon of property law to be "seized of the entirety" rather than "taking by respective moieties [parts]." But if each spouse owns all the estate, then strict logic would seem to dictate the paradox that while the property's owner cannot convey or indebt the land without the consent of the property's owner, neither can the property's owner stop the property's owner from selling or indebting that which, after all, belongs to the property's owner.

In deciding *Sawada v. Endo*, the court attempts to navigate this conceptual muddle through the straightforward use of circular reasoning. It first quotes another court to the effect that "each spouse owns the whole [estate] while both live" and that "at the death of either the other continues to own the whole, and does not acquire any new interest from the other." From its witnessing of this metaphysical marvel the court "deduces the indivisibility and unseverability of the estate into two interests, and hence that the creditors of either spouse cannot during their joint lives reach by execution any interest which the debtor had in land so held." Impressed by the force of its own deductive powers, the court then muses that while "one may have doubts as to whether the holding of land by entireties is advisable or in harmony with the spirit of the legislation in favor of married women," these doubts must give way before the insight that "when such an estate is created due effect must be given to its peculiar characteristics."

Here we see the more or less hypnotic power that formal—or, more precisely, pseudo-formal—modes of reasoning continue to cast over the workings of the legal mind. (The reasoning in this case can't be formal in any useful sense because of that conceptual pluralism, acknowledged by the court in its review of the laws of various states, that results in conflicting conceptualizations of the modern tenancy by the entireties.) Yet the Supreme Court of Hawaii gives no indication whatsoever that it has the faintest suspicion there might be anything fishy about this particular use of deductive reasoning. Indeed, the idea that they are simply begging the question seems quite beyond the judges' collective ken. It is as if a painter, asked why he always made his unicorns white when other artists chose to represent those imaginary beasts as black or green, were to reply that he had always found whiteness to be a "peculiar characteristic" of the unicorn's actual coloration.

When the court turns from discussing legal concepts to instrumental considerations of policy, we receive even clearer confirmation that we are in the presence of a level of cognitive confusion akin to that accompanying some sort of mental illness. The argument that it is unfair to creditors to exempt the tenancy from the debts of either spouse is dismissed with the observation that "If the debt arose prior to the creation of the estate, the property was not a basis of credit, and if the debt arose subsequently the creditor presumably had notice of the characteristics of the estate which limited his right to reach the property." The court then criticizes by implication the choices supposedly made by the plaintiffs in the case before it, pointing out that "there is obviously nothing to prevent the creditor from insisting upon the subjection of property held in a tenancy by the entirety as a condition precedent to the extension of credit."

These kinds of statements should give teachers of law pause. Do we have the misfortune to be burdened with the task of subjecting some number of mentally impaired persons to the benefits of legal education, or is it perhaps the case that those "benefits" are in fact doing serious damage to the cognitive capacities of persons of otherwise normal intelligence?* How is it possible for these judges to entirely overlook problems of fairness created by the existence of involuntary creditors, *when the plaintiffs in the case before them are representatives of that very class*? And how is it possible for this court to assume that even voluntary creditors "presumably had notice" of the

---

*Note that the state supreme court judges who decided *Sawada v. Endo* were quite far advanced in the American legal hierarchy. It is therefore difficult to dismiss the opinion as a product of *mere* incompetence on the part of marginal legal actors.

relevant characteristics of the tenancy by the entireties in this particular legal context when, after all, the court is *creating* those same
characteristics by means of this very decision?

After some further discussion of various public policy justifications for ruling as it has, the specious character of the court's reasoning achieves a sort of Platonic perfection when it concludes its
analysis with the following remarkable announcement:

> If we were to select between a public policy favoring the creditors of
> one of the spouses and one favoring the interests of the family unit, we
> would not hesitate to choose the latter. *But we need not make this choice*
> for, as we pointed out earlier, by the very nature of the tenancy by the
> entirety as we view it, "a . . . broad immunity from claims of separate
> creditors remains among its vital interests." [emphasis added]

The opinion in *Sawada v. Endo* can be reduced to the following
propositions.

1. Legal concept X is conceptualized in a number of different ways
in the context of situation Y, thus producing result A in Jurisdiction
One, result B in Jurisdiction Two, result C in Jurisdiction Three,
and result D in Jurisdiction Four.

2. Legal concept X has never been conceptualized in the context of
situation Y in Jurisdiction Five.

3. In Jurisdiction Five, legal concept X must be conceptualized in
the context of situation Y to produce result C.

4. This conceptualization is impelled on the decision maker not
because the result it produces is in some way desirable, but rather
because this result is inherent in the proper conceptualization of
legal concept X in the context of situation Y in Jurisdiction Five.
Q.E.D.

This is the kind of thing that drove the classic legal realists—anti-
formalist legal scholars of the 1920s and 1930s—into paroxysms of
rage and disgust. Sixty years later, despite routine legal academic
claims that "we" are all realists now, anyone who practices law is
well aware that such blatantly circular forms of pseudo-formal rea-

soning are still an integral part of actual legal decision making. *Sawada v. Endo* is a far from uncommon demonstration of what happens when a particularly clumsy magician struggles in full view of his audience to stuff a recalcitrant rabbit into a too-small hat, and then—having at last succeeded—proceeds with an air of absurdly triumphant pride to lift the enraged bunny high aloft, so that all may look on his handiwork with amazement and awe.

At this point, the sophisticated contemporary law professor is supposed to declare such transparent sophistry anathema and proceed to do—what? The modern instrumental orthodoxy taught in American law schools proclaims that disputes that are conceptually indeterminate should be decided on the basis of social policy or, more ostentatiously, "principle." (I should emphasize that this instrumental orthodoxy is less universal than some of my arguments would seem to imply. Many American legal academics still deny—as both the implicit beliefs of conventionally minded doctrinalists, and the explicit assertions of jurisprudential luminaries such as Ronald Dworkin illustrate—that legal disputes are *ever* conceptually indeterminate.) But again, such disputes are formally indeterminate precisely *because* the relevant legal concepts reflect powerfully conflicting social policies and principles. Beneath its tendentious conceptual veneer *Sawada v. Endo* is about the clash between the libertarian championing of the value of freedom of contract and the communitarian impulse to protect the family from the recklessness of a single member; between the desire to keep credit cheap and thus widely available, and to maintain those economic privileges granted to those who undertake marriage and child-rearing; between the urge to compensate the victims of unfortunate accidents and to avoid magnifying the social damage such accidents cause. Our fear of the ineliminable practical and theoretical difficulties posed by the attempt to mediate these essential tensions allows us to delude ourselves into believing we can somehow do so—if, that is, the best minds of our generation will first think very, very carefully about such problems, and then proceed to exercise "good judgment," "practical reason," or, in Ronald Dworkin's formulation, "the best available political theory."

Let us consider briefly how well Dworkin—the most masterful illusionist in the field—actually succeeds in the performance of this phantasmagoric task.

Smaller Rabbits, Bigger Hats

Despite his reputation as an esoteric legal philosopher, Ronald Dworkin is in all truth a lawyer's lawyer: a supremely skillful rhetorician whose silky arguments subtly flatter the political prejudices of *bien pensant* readers of the *New York Review*, even as he drapes those arguments in the academic robes of the Empire of Reason and the Constitution of Principle. Thus in his book *Life's Dominion*, Dworkin plausibly reduces the vexed moral question of abortion rights to a clash of essentially religious worldviews concerning the "sacred" status of life, and then argues that significant government regulation of abortion would violate the establishment clause of the First Amendment. Now as an initial matter this argument is plausible only because the seductive eloquence of Dworkin's prose hides from the great bulk of his readers various inconvenient details, such as the fact that Dworkin's definition of what counts as a "religious belief" is much broader than that recognized by modern judicial decisions interpreting the establishment clause. An even more intellectually problematic difficulty is avoided when Dworkin conceals from his readership any hint that accepting these modern establishment clause doctrines as correct also requires—as all candid supporters of the doctrines admit—that the interpreter also accept a radically ahistorical understanding of the clause's meaning.*

*It is no longer in serious question that the historical purpose of the establishment clause was to leave the governmental support of religion—up to and including the establishment of official state religions—to the states themselves, rather than to the federal government. See Steven D. Smith's *Foreordained Failure* for a full account. Dworkin's failure to acknowledge this difficulty should be all the more startling if we consider that his theory of constitutional interpretation claims, at least in part, to be concerned explicitly with the demands of historical understanding. See Ronald Dworkin, *Law's Empire*, at 230, 338, 380.

Dworkin's argument thus simply ignores the entire problem of conceptual incommensurability in constitutional interpretation: the interpretive and intellectual crises caused by the circumstance that the American legal system gives conceptually incommensurable, yet still supposedly authoritative answers to the question of whether the meaning of the Constitution is determined by its text, or by certain interpretations of that text. Indeed the Constitution as a whole (as opposed to judicial decisions that *refer to* the Constitution) appears to have nothing whatever to say about a right to abortion, or to privacy, or individual autonomy, or sacredness, or any of the other highly abstract concepts that make up the heart of Dworkin's argument.

Furthermore, Dworkin's argument only succeeds if we accept it as axiomatic that prior to viability a fetus is not a constitutionally protected person (Dworkin admits that states can prohibit abortion once the fetus is viable). We must treat this assertion as an axiom because Dworkin's book provides no explanation as to *why* a fetus is not in fact such a person. And, if we consider the essentially metaphysical and indeed rather mystical character of the concept of "personhood," we will realize there is no reason to imagine the book *could* provide such an explanation. Thus Dworkin is reduced to asserting that the central holding of the key abortion cases, *Roe v. Wade*, and *Planned Parenthood v. Casey*—that a purported constitutional right to procreative autonomy forbids states from regulating almost all abortions—"follows from *any competent interpretation* of the due process clause and of the Supreme Court's [other] decisions applying it" [emphasis added].

As any competent interpreter of American constitutional law will recognize—at least any whose cognitive faculties haven't been hopelessly impaired by the ideological distortion surrounding this issue—Dworkin's central interpretive claim is so absurd that it doesn't warrant the dignity of a serious reply. Richard Posner's acid dismissal of the linchpin of Dworkin's argument more than suffices: "This amounts to saying that the thousands of lawyers, many of them highly expert and distinguished and several of them Justices of the U.S. Supreme Court, who believe that the abortion cases do *not* follow from a competent interpretation of the due process clause and of due process jurisprudence are—incompetent, maybe even deluded."*

That Dworkin's disingenuous use of strongly conclusory reasoning fools as many people as it does is a tribute to his rhetorical gifts: which is to say to his skill in obscuring the vigorous leaps of unjustified faith required by his argument. But the effectiveness of those gifts is in turn enabled by a powerful need on the part of his audience: the need to believe that the most difficult moral, political, and legal questions can be resolved through the use of reason, especially what is called "legal reason." Still, even if a magician is so skillful that no one in the audience can explain how the rabbit got into the hat, only the children present truly believe that it was done by magic. For all legal rhetoric's grandiloquent talk of "reason" and "principle," we know that *our* law is always a contingent product of fallible human choices—choices that within interpretive equilibrium zones must remain essentially contestable. It is thus inevitable that whenever they are deployed in such situations, the most sophisticated political and philosophical arguments will in the end be every bit as axiom-ridden and tautological as was *Sawada v. Endo's* crude resort to a more obviously circular, pseudo-formal line of reasoning.

Toward a General Theory of Unicorns

The need to believe in the power of reason in general, and of legal reason in particular, plays an important role in producing that extremely complex and interesting psychological phenomenon, the modern legal mind. Of course it may be more than a little ridiculous to speak of "the" modern legal mind; but nevertheless at the risk of serious overgeneralization I will try to trace out some of its characteristic features.

Two attitudes toward the ontological status of unicorns seem rela-

---

*Of course in a sense I go Dworkin one better by claiming that *both* sides in this particular legal argument are deluded. But I locate the delusion in the search for "the" legal answer to such questions, rather than in the giving of some particular answer.

tively unproblematic. One could, for example, believe that unicorns are actual biological phenomena—that unicorns are real in the same way horses are real. Or one could believe that unicorns are creations of the human mind, imaginary creatures whose characteristics are therefore wholly a product of our assumptions about those same characteristics. Now imagine a social practice that requires persons to act as if they sincerely believe there actually are independent facts of the matter regarding unicorns—facts not dependent on human beliefs—and indeed routinely requires these people to assert the existence of such facts. Yet suppose this practice also requires that on certain occasions those who engage in the practice claim no such independent facts concerning the status of unicorns exist because, after all, "everyone knows" unicorns are merely products of the human mind. We could anticipate that many of the participants in this practice will develop a sort of double consciousness about unicorns, one in which they will both affirm and deny—and in which they will in a sense both believe and not believe—that unicorns are actual or imaginary creatures, depending on the context in which such affirmation or denial, and belief or absence of belief, is deemed appropriate.

The participants in this practice would as a matter of psychological necessity have to engage in a kind of Orwellian doublethink. On certain occasions, they would argue passionately about what colors unicorns really were, or about their actual population, whereabouts, and habits. On other occasions they would treat with derision anyone who could be foolish enough to take the naive view that unicorns were the sort of creatures that existed outside the minds of the men and women who imagined them into being. On yet other occasions they would seem to assert both views at once, claiming that while of course unicorns didn't really exist outside our imaginations, nevertheless by treating them *as if* they were actual living animals we could eliminate any practical distinction between the characteristics of real and imaginary creatures.

Such is the ordinary mental condition of the modern American lawyer. The modern lawyer, and especially the modern judge and law professor, must continually practice a sort of "as if" jurisprudence, within the context of which the lawyer both knows and doesn't know that most important legal facts are facts only to the extent we believe them to *be* legal facts. Various strategies are then employed to deal with the intense cognitive dissonance that characterizes this condition. A common one among practicing lawyers is to simply ignore the dissonance—to treat it as someone else's problem. That someone else is, of course, whatever decision maker is precluded from employing the same cognitive strategy by virtue of the decision maker's decisional responsibilities. Among judges the strategy exemplified by the opinion in *Sawada v. Endo*—that of failing altogether to grasp the interpretive complexities of the situation—remains a perennial favorite. As I often have occasion to explain to my students, if a judge undertakes a sufficiently rigorous mortification of the intellect every decision can eventually become "an easy case."

Although this latter gambit is far from unknown among law professors, the more sophisticated legal academic prefers to affect a jaded, world-weary cynicism. You see, "we" know all this already; there's nothing new here; Wittgenstein or Holmes or Lord Coke or William of Occam said exactly the same thing; indeed this very same heresy is in many respects identical to that denial of consubstantiality first proclaimed by Arius and duly extirpated at the Council of Nicaea, etc., etc. No doubt. But note well: let some rare issue that still engages the ebbing passions of our cynic arise, let the Supreme Court touch on the scholar's ideological *bête noire*, or the local zoning board threaten to put a McDonald's across the street from his house, and all that postmodern ennui in the face of the circulation of social power, all that intellectual indifference to what in another mood are treated as nothing but endlessly recursive, essentially meaningless language games goes right out the window. Suddenly notions of "the rule of law," of "fundamental concepts of justice and fairness," and even of "the correct decision in this case" spring, vampire-like, back to a kind of morbid life. Professor X, who on most days sounds like a cross between a Chicago alderman and Michel Foucault, is transmogrified into a hybrid of Perry Mason and Christopher Columbus Langdell, and duly unleashes a torrent of sanctimonious formalism in the service of his rediscovered ethical zeal.

Still, I must admit there is something unreal, and even unfair, about these criticisms. Fundamental concepts of fairness require that I consider the possibility that if I had to kill, cage, and impoverish people on a regular basis—if, that is, I had to actually "do" law, as opposed to merely *talking about* doing law—then I, too, might succeed in dumbing myself down to the level of the *Sawada* court.* If it were my job to parcel out, on the basis of circular justifications and instrumental guesses, a daily portion of the violence of the state, I, too, might become extremely adept at maintaining the intense levels of sophisticated doublethink that get the normatively committed law professor through the day. Perhaps the proper function of a legal education really is to produce persons who "think like lawyers": individuals, that is, who are trained to hold various unambivalent yet rationally unjustified beliefs, necessary for the vigorous deployment of social power, that nevertheless remain highly role specific, and are therefore subject to change at a moment's—or a client's—notice. Such beliefs help mold otherwise ordinary people into the sorts of state actors who will not hesitate to kill, cage, and impoverish their fellow citizens on what are deemed institutionally appropriate occasions, in much the same way that successful military training renders otherwise pacific young men capable of committing acts of politically sanctioned homicide.

The Ministry of Law

In Orwell's *Nineteen Eighty-Four* there is a particularly chilling scene in which, after the director of the Ministry of Love has subjected Winston Smith to intense physical tortures, he employs yet another strategy in the process of Smith's gradual re-education.

> "This time it will not hurt," [O'Brien] said. "Keep your eyes fixed on mine."

---

*"The very construction of judges—that which enables them to be judges at all—will lead them in important senses not to see, not to understand, and not to pursue certain lines of inquiry." Pierre Schlag, "Clerks in the Maze" in Paul F. Campos, Pierre Schlag, and Steven D. Smith, *Against the Law*.

At this moment there was a devastating explosion, or what seemed like an explosion. . . . A terrific, painless blow had flattened [Smith] out. Also something had happened inside his head . . . somewhere or other there was a large patch of emptiness, as though a piece had been taken out of his brain.

"It will not last," said O'Brien. "Look at me in the eyes. . . . Just now I held up the fingers of my hand to you. You saw five fingers. Do you remember that?"

"Yes."

O'Brien held up the fingers of his left hand, with the thumb concealed.

"There are five fingers there. Do you see five fingers?"

"Yes."

And he did see them, for a fleeting instant . . . there had been a moment—he did not know how long, thirty seconds, perhaps—of luminous certainty, when each new suggestion of O'Brien's had filled up a patch of emptiness and become absolute truth, and when two and two could have been three as easily as five, if that were what was needed . . .

"You see now," said O'Brien, "that it is at any rate possible."

Compare this passage to Karl Llewellyn's famous description of the student's first year of law school: "The hardest job of the first year is to lop off your commonsense, to knock your ethics into temporary anesthesia. Your view of social policy, your sense of justice—to knock these out of you along with woozy thinking, along with ideas all fuzzed along their edges."

But of course when we undertake the resolution of hard issues it will always be the case that the relevant legal concepts, the demands of social policy, and the ideal of justice will by necessity appear to sensitive interpreters to be "fuzzed along their edges." That very same formal, empirical, and ethical fuzziness is, after all, what makes hard issues hard. A successful legal education therefore both sharpens and desensitizes the adept's sense of analytic complexity, sharpening it so that the advocate can identify various plausible arguments, and then deadening it for the purpose of making and (especially) deciding between such arguments. This characteristic doubleness of the legal mind produces the doubleness of the literal *sophomore*—of the brilliant simpleton who understands and exploits and at appropriate times forgets—the evidentiary problems, conceptual incommensurabilities, and ethical dilemmas that always characterize difficult legal issues. To be trained to think like a lawyer is to be taught how to evoke all the chaotic complexity of law, and then how to repress the intolerable doubt that same evocation can produce by going on to achieve the "luminous certainty" required of the advocate or judge.

Within an even vaguely democratic culture, laws must be compromises between widely held yet conflicting social norms, which is to say that they will be, at best, the honest hunches of all-too-human people attempting to deal with profound ethical disagreement, and to resolve the inevitable social conflicts this disagreement engenders. Indeed, the modern metaphysical crisis of belief that Nietzsche so clearly identified has combined with the ever-more evident limits of rational inquiry to leave us in a situation where it often appears that, if God is not dead, then at the least he has left humanity blind. For even if we assume that God (or whatever god-term fulfills the deity's indispensable role within what Kenneth Burke has called the "coy theology" of secular metaphysics) really does provide answers to our ultimate questions, this information must evidently remain unavailable to the moral man.

In our culture law does its work by being the peculiar kind of psychological artifact that is treated simultaneously as if it both does and does not have some sort of formal existence independent of our desires and beliefs. Indeed, this psychologically complex "as if" quality of legal reasoning remains so deeply tangled within the rationalization structures of the legal mind that our cultural ideal of law may simply be inseparable from some semiconscious illusion of legal objectivity. The law remains for modern Americans an essentially mythical beast: which is to say it is the kind of half-acknowledged cultural fiction that retains a much greater power than many a self-evident truth. For even we who are disenchanted—who have seen the magician's incantations fail a few too many times—cannot hear the hoofbeats of his unicorn without falling, if only for a moment, beneath their potent spell.

7

ADDICTED TO LAW

In the course of the life struggle, efforts and results are
found not to be in strict relation, though the correspondence is regular enough so that people depend on
it.... Man's reaction to this element of chance has
taken two forms. He has tried to dominate it, thus giving rise to the phenomena of science and the development of skill. Or he has accepted it as hopelessly beyond
control and courted it, thus giving rise to the phenomena of magic....

DAVID D. ALLEN, *The Nature of Gambling*

The President of the United States is about to step onto the tarmac
of Denver's brand-new airport, where he will deliver a campaign
speech, framed artfully for the cameras against a backdrop of purple
mountain majesty. After crossing cities and plains, deserts and
mighty rivers, he has descended out of the clouds to bring us a message of hope, and to show us how to build a bridge that will reach
the ever-receding future. Now he emerges from his ceremonial air-
ship, to be greeted by kowtowing dignitaries, high school cheer-
leaders, crowds of the curious and the committed, and of course
that swarm of equipment-laden journalists forever trailing in his
charismatic wake. He speaks the words he has come all this way to
deliver, words designed to be the first sound bite on this evening's
national news: "Today I have signed legislation to crack down on
illegal drugs."

A wave of cheers engulfs the podium, above which—barely visible
behind a medusa-like amalgamation of microphones—we get a

glimpse of perfectly coifed hair, and of an eminently presidential expression, stern yet empathic, noble yet sincere.

This exercise represents what in contemporary America gets called "politics." Still, despite our jaded ennui—despite all the seemingly bottomless reservoirs of cynicism so characteristic of these times—no one appears to notice the most remarkable feature of the President's statement. Reporters will duly note he is signing this legislation in response to his opponent's claims that he is soft on drugs. Law and order types will dismiss the action as "playing politics," refusing to believe that this President, redolent as he is of easy virtue, can really be serious about doing what it takes to fight the war on drugs. By contrast those of a libertarian inclination will deplore yet another incursion on our constitutionally-guaranteed freedoms, and see in the President's remarks another example of that brazen opportunism for which he is famed. Still, the most salient feature of the President's carefully scripted utterance goes unremarked—its sheer absurdity.

Nearly two decades ago the federal government began to pass a torrent of anti-drug legislation, featuring stiffer penalties, mandatory sentences, the elimination of parole, and other draconian elements intended to combat a perceived social crisis brought on by the use of illegal mind-altering substances. Indeed, several of the new laws Congress enacted declared that the goal of these statuties was no less than to make America "a drug-free nation" by the end of the 1990s. (If we dismiss such statements as mere rhetoric, we are ignoring that such rhetoric has real consequences). Today, primarily as a result of these laws, the prison population of the United States has more than doubled since the mid-1980s, and nearly quadrupled since 1975. More than half of all federal prisoners now incarcerated are serving drug-related sentences; the average length of these sentences is by far the longest in the developed world. Meanwhile, the wholesale price of cocaine and heroin is actually lower than it was fifteen years ago; drug use among teenagers has skyrocketed; and drugs are as widely available as ever. For example, in California, despite more than a billion dollars spent on attempts to eradicate the farming of marijuana plants, marijuana growers continue to har-

vest their crops with impunity, and law enforcement officials now
admit openly there is not much they can do about it.

Faced with these sorts of facts, disinterested observers of the situation admit the so-called "war on drugs" has been an almost complete failure. Indeed, given the characteristics of the enemy, it is
fairly remarkable anyone ever believed it could be won. Among
those characteristics are: the employment of mind-altering substances in all known human cultures; the huge profits always generated by underground economies in highly desirable contraband, and
the enormous incentives to participation in those economies such
profits produce; the total impossibility of stopping or even impeding
significantly the importation of banned substances into a country
with thousands of miles of unguarded borders; and, not least, that
cautionary tale of spectacular failure, the federal government's
attempt to ban the sale of alcohol during what in retrospect are
remembered as "the roaring Twenties."

Given all this, it would in truth make more sense for the President to announce he has undertaken to perform a ritualistic dance,
designed to drive away the evil drug spirits, than for him to inform
us that he has yet again "signed legislation to crack down on illegal
drugs." After all it is just conceivable, empirically speaking, that
the Evil Drug Spirit Dance might work; and at the very least it
would represent a low-cost experiment in social policy. We *know*
the legislation isn't going to work; and we also know it will merely
continue to add to the expense of a set of destructive policy initia-
tives that are not only utter failures, but are costing us a fortune to
implement.

None of these points are even particularly controversial. Why
then is the President's proposal not met with hoots of derisive
laughter, or perhaps with a grave suggestion that he be examined, so
as to determine the cause of this delusional pattern of thought?
Why is the reaction of his opponent instead to claim the legislation
doesn't go far enough, and to promise that he, if elected, will do
even more along these same lines? Why, in short, is the answer to an
important social problem almost always *more law*, even or rather

especially in those social contexts where the evidence more or less shouts at us that more law isn't going to work? Doing a rain dance in the tropics: this I can understand. But in the desert? Why do we trust so blindly in the weak magic of law?

You Need Therapy

Americans like to think that problems have solutions, and hence they tend to regard culturally sanctioned expertise with something approaching superstitious awe. Few better examples of this tendency can be found than that peculiar icon of our popular culture, the advice column. My personal favorite in the genre is America's as well: that venerable dispenser of the timeless platitude, Ann Landers. Every morning, after reading the box scores and the betting line, I join millions of my fellow citizens by turning to her column, where she reigns like some sort of cultural concierge over the world of the American bourgeoisie.

Here we will find personal tales of woe ranging from the trivial to the tragic, from the neighborly conflict engendered by a barking dog to the psychological devastation wrought by lust, violence, betrayal, and cruelty. Two themes consistently dominate Ann's responses: her respect for the various experts she consults, and her unlimited faith in the efficacy of "counseling." To read Ann Landers regularly is to become aware that she considers no possible dimension of human tragedy, no conflict laden with unspeakable burdens of grief and suffering, to be in principle immune from the professional blandishments of the therapist. Here are just a few examples from a recent three-month period. A little girl is raped by her father and yet is still required by the law to visit him twice a week: "Get Sherry into counseling at once. . . ." Another woman is haunted by a childhood full of violence and abuse: "I hope you are getting counseling to help deal with your nightmarish past." A Texas reader writes a letter expressing her shock and horror at a group of local children, ages eight to fourteen, who beat a horse to death for the sheer fun of it. Ann's response? "The parents or guardians of these children should be made, by law, to attending several counseling sessions. These children need special attention from mental health professionals as well." A woman discovers that her husband is having an affair with her own sister: "I strongly recommend that you and your husband get joint counseling."

Of course Ann's advice merely reflects contemporary mores. In America today, as supposedly scientific modes of discourse replace religion in the cultural business of purveying metaphysical answers to life's most difficult questions, the therapist has gradually displaced the clergyman as the dispenser of all-purpose practical wisdom. Indeed it has now become routine to send, along with search and rescue teams and medical supplies, platoons of self-proclaimed "grief counselors" to the sites of great public disasters. (For my part, I've never been able to imagine what kind of "counseling" could possibly help a mother who has just realized that the child she will never see again has died a horrible and apparently meaningless death. Others, it seems, have better imaginations than mine.)

Ann's worship of therapists and their counseling skills also goes hand in hand with her—and the culture's—generalized fetish for medicine men of all varieties. With the decay of belief in personal immortality comes the sacralization of these modern shamans of the tribe who, god-like, seem to hold in their hands the keys to life and death themselves. As part of the professionalization of this sector of the secular priesthood, a Cartesian division of labor has taken place: one in which the therapist has become the doctor of the soul, who through the magic of science cures those spiritual ills that before were thought to be the province of the ceremonies and sacraments of the Church. In their playing of this role, therapists fulfill part of the broader culture's demand for some sort of expert class that will provide answers to otherwise unanswerable existential questions.

Sometimes, when I contemplate that there are still Americans alive today whose parents were slaves, I try to imagine which of our own cultural practices will engender equivalent shudders of horror and disgust in our descendants. Along these lines, we might want to reconsider the practice of unveiling the most intimate secrets of our lives to total strangers, so that they may then analyze our deepest motives and most profound fears, and thus help us to alter the essence of our personalities in ways thought socially desirable. It is just possible that, when seen from a historical distance, such procedures will not be surrounded by quite the same benign glow that tends to envelop them today.

For instance, I have a neighbor—let us call him Humbert—whose domestic arrangements have been so spectacularly irregular that— even in these supremely tolerant times, even in our ideally atomized subdivision of anonymous houses—he has become a figure of communal gossip and speculation. Humbert moved into the house he now occupies eighteen months ago, in the midst of divorcing his second wife, upon whose body he had sired a boy, now three years old. He brought with him a very young woman, pregnant with what was assumed to be his second child. Within three months of the birth of a baby girl the newborn's mother had, it was said, been forced to depart the Humbert residence with the new baby in tow. Almost immediately upon their departure Humbert began cohabiting with a yet younger girleen, a sylph-like creature whom at present he appears to be keeping in some state of obscure concubinage. As for Humbert's means of support, he is during working hours transformed into—guess, reader, guess!—a fully certified, state-approved, "licensed personal counselor."

Fortunately, despite the growing dominance of the culture of therapeutic, powerful critiques of modern therapeutic ideology have been put forth in recent years by writers as diverse as Philip Rieff, Thomas Szasz, and Alasdair MacIntyre. These critics point to how those who undertake bureaucratically directed managerial roles must obliterate the distinction between manipulative and nonmanipulative social relations, as well as to how therapists accomplish the same sort of obliteration in the sphere of personal life. In each of these cases the search for truth is replaced with the quest for technique; and disputes about proper ends are subsumed into arguments about the effective pursuit of those ends. Within such a world, moral argument appears to give way to value-neutral "expertise" precisely because the significant moral questions have already been begged by the rational-bureaucratic structure of the decision process itself. But what if as a matter of fact these forms of rational-bureaucratic expertise have *no* value for the purpose of determining how we should deal with the most profound questions and conflicts that trouble our moral lives?

The basic professional role dilemmas of the therapist and of the modern lawyer are thus very similar. Each operates within a social discourse in which he or she is expected—at least tacitly and often explicitly—to be able to answer the most difficult questions of personal and political obligation. But of course the professional expertise each actually possesses, useful though it may be for more limited purposes, turns out to have no relevance whatsoever to the resolution of such profoundly existential questions. Yet precisely because they are placed in the absurd position of being expected to "do something" about problems that defeat the powers of their professional knowledge, people who play the social roles required of such experts develop the habit of identifying *the claim* they are undertaking efficacious action with *the fact* of such action taking place. So it is that the various "talking cures" that make up psychotherapy continue to represent themselves as supposedly therapeutic social practices, despite slender evidence that they are in fact consistently therapeutic, even within the narrow range of results those practices define as representing therapeutic effectiveness.

Similarly, legal actors come to identify "doing something" about social problems with the undertaking of various types of legal action. Eventually the gap between the representations of the practice regarding what the practice is accomplishing and the actual accomplishments of the practice can become so stark that many legal utterances can only be understood as taking place within the context of some elaborate form of magical thinking. Consider in this light the President's statement that he had "cracked down" on illegal drug use by the act of signing yet another piece of prohibitive legislation. The routine quality of this sort of statement inures us to the elementary insight that there is at best only a very weak relationship between the acts of signing criminal legislation aimed at the drug trade, and of doing something efficacious about illegal drug use.* Yet as we will see, law is not the only area of modern life where the distinctions between, on the one hand, a belief in science and rationality, and on the other, a faith in what is thought of as religion or magic are a good deal less clear than we are usually led to believe.

Law, Science, and Magic

I live in the city of Louisville, Colorado. Once a mildy notorious mining town, home to most of the bars and all the brothels of Boulder County, it has since been transformed into a typical bedroom community of suburban commuters. Because many of its more civic-minded residents are professional-class refugees from more or less Hobbesian urban environments, the city government these residents control will often produce regulatory proclamations that give evidence of the sorts of anxieties to which people with these types of backgrounds are prone. Even as humble a text as the Louisville Public Library Code of Conduct is an impressively comprehensive document, the interpretation of which provides us with an indirect glimpse of various urban pathologies that continue to fester in late twentieth-century America.

After a verbose preamble, which among other things informs us helpfully that "behavior becomes unacceptable when it infringes on the rights of others," the code provides thirty-one examples of unacceptable conduct. These examples can be sorted into five general categories:

---

*Or consider the argument for a balanced budget amendment, which boils down to the belief that the best way to ensure legislators pass legislation that balances the federal budget is to pass legislation requiring legislators to pass legislation that balances the federal budget.

1. Highly site-specific regulations (i.e., "Eating or Drinking," "Overcrowding at Study Tables or Carrels (limit of 4 per study table").

2. Behavior associated with street people ("Bathing/Washing Clothes," "Lack of Shoes or Shirt," "Loitering including refusal to leave at closing").

3. Behavior evincing failures of basic acculturation mechanisms ("Obscene Language," "Body Odor/Perfume/Cologne (Excessive) which Elicits General Complaint or Causes Discomfort to Other Library Users," "Excessive Public Displays of Affection").

4. General criminal behavior ("Theft," "Gambling" "Physical, Sexual or Verbal Abuse or Harassment of Library Users or Staff").

5. Criminalized behavior associated with mental illness or substance abuse ("Exhibitionism/Flashing," "Visible Drug or Alcohol Intoxication," "Voyeurism/Peeping").

After the list of specific examples the Code of Conduct concludes with the American lawyer's equivalent of the old anti-Soviet slander provision in the USSR's criminal code: "Any unlawful behavior and any other behavior that unreasonably interferes with the safe or reasonable use of the library by other persons."

This code, posted as it is in prominent places all around the building, is of course a very ordinary document of the kind found throughout the public spaces of contemporary America. Normally, neither you nor I would give it more than a glance; and we almost surely wouldn't spare it a second thought. Yet it is in its own quotidian way a remarkable text. Let us attempt to comprehend both the specific ideological commitments and the general worldview to which it tacitly testifies.

Orthodox American rule of law ideology demands that those actions the state has prohibited be made public so that persons may have an opportunity to inform themselves as to what is and is not allowed. Once this condition has been met people may then be held to "know the law"—ignorance of it being, famously, no excuse. It follows from this that when persons fail to conform their conduct to the law it can be assumed they are "choosing" to violate its publicly announced requirements. The key elements in this particular ideological justification of the exercise of state power are thus publicity, knowledge, and volition.

Such at least is the theory. How well does this theory apply to a typical piece of modern bureaucratic regulation? Of the types of behavior the Louisville library code prohibits, we might note that only those listed in the first category can be thought to convey useful information to any minimally socialized member of the community. I admit there could be a real question as to whether I'm allowed to bring a bag of pretzels into the library, but do I really require "notice" that I can't snatch purses, expose myself to patrons, do my laundry in the bathroom, or play high-stakes poker in the reference area? Suppose I hadn't been given notice of any of these things; does it follow I'm free to claim as a defense insufficient publicity on the part of the state? Must, that is, the authorities first inform me of the specific rules they intend to enforce before they interfere with what in a world without public legal notices to that effect will be considered my presumptive right to physically, verbally, and sexually abuse library patrons and workers?

Can there be any nonpsychotic person of minimally functional intelligence who would suppose that *any* of the things on this list, other than those dealt with in the most site-specific regulations, were not prohibited? Of course all social rules include areas of vagueness (which public displays of affection are "excessive?"), but these borderline problems can hardly be cured by posting general proscriptions of the type found in public legal notices. So here we seem to be faced with a wholly superfluous invocation of legal rules: rules that merely reflect tacit social understandings that themselves have no apparent need to be cast into a public legal text. But the actual interpretive situation is still more peculiar than this.

Note that ultimately the supposed purpose of the library code is to give persons the knowledge they need to exercise a freely willed choice to follow the law. That is, the idea must be that people who would otherwise engage in acts of voyeurism, or who would stumble into the Louisville Public Library under the influence of crack cocaine, will duly note they are prohibited from doing so, and will therefore choose to refrain from indulging in such legally pro-scribed behavior. These assumptions are, to put it as charitably as possible, unwarranted. There is no evidence whatsoever that people in the grip of sexual compulsions or substance addictions need to be informed their behavior is unacceptable; indeed, in the case of voyeurism and exhibitionism, the very unacceptability of the behav-ior is what sexualizes and thus enables it. And there is also no real evidence that legally prohibiting such behavior has a significant effect on the "choice"—if it can even be thought of usefully *as* a choice—to engage in or avoid the prohibited conduct. Here, in the social subtext of the most ordinary legal rules, we get a glimpse of the ideology of the autonomous liberal self gone haywire.

The library's code of conduct also illustrates the characteristic hypertrophy of modern legal reasoning. It is not that legal concepts such as "notice" and "choice" never make sense; in fact, most of the time they do. It is rather that we tend to employ these sorts of con-cepts so promiscuously that we lose sight of the relative lack of salience they have to many social situations. We have seen how, in the context of anti-drug legislation, the common-sense insight that attaching bad consequences to certain actions often deters persons from undertaking those actions is exaggerated out of all reasonable proportion. In a similar vein, the modest idea that talking about their problems sometimes makes people feel better gets blown up into the grand scientific and cultural pretensions of psychothera-peutic ideology. Much like these former examples, the library code illustrates some of the ways in which otherwise useful modes of analysis can be pushed to a point where the hypertrophied character of what is called "reason" becomes indistinguishable from a form of magical thinking.

Posting a public notice of the unacceptability of theft, or of exhi-bitionism, or of physical and sexual abuse, is very much like passing yet another law providing still more penalties for the sale of already illegal drugs. Such actions represent our legal culture's equivalent to the practice of nailing garlic over doorways to repel vampires. In each case a psychological imperative born of a sense of lack of control, and of the fear and anxiety this sensation produces, demands of us that we "do something." Those same factors then lead us to do things that appear in the cold light of rational analysis to be almost wholly irrational.

Now admittedly the psychological placebo effect they may induce in some observers might serve as a potential justification for undertaking such apparently pointless rituals. Other explanations remain available as well: the supposed "notice" function of the regulations can be explained as an attempt to protect against potential liability from thieves, and so on. Yet note how such explanations are still parasitic on the idea that this "notice" function has a practical effect: otherwise why would it work as a psychological placebo or protect against liability? Or the regulations might be interpreted as a community statement of moral belief, with no particular instrumental function. But before we embrace some sort of optimistic Durkheimian account, celebrating the functionally necessary role our often irrational faith in the power of reason plays in the maintenance of important cultural practices, let us first examine that faith in a more troubling interpretive context.

Recently, an extreme case of obsessive behavior was processed through the court system of a large American city. Tom Davis met Linda Jones* at their mutual workplace in a neighboring state. For a time they socialized at work together—eating lunch and so forth—until Jones, who was involved in a romantic relationship with another man, tried to discontinue any association with Davis, who had begun to display signs of becoming obsessed with her. Jones then moved out of the state, and enrolled in a graduate program in the city where her case would eventually be processed. She soon discovered that Davis had followed her, and had in fact moved into the same apartment complex. At this point Davis began to engage in a classic pattern of relentless stalking behavior: he left books on her

---

*I have changed the names of the people involved; all other assertions are taken from court records.

doorstep, followed her to school, bicycled and drove past places where she worked, and tried to rent apartments near her workplaces. Jones went to court and obtained a restraining order against Davis, which he ignored. Finally, Davis tunneled his way underneath the apartment complex and drilled a hole in Jones' bathroom floor. When she discovered the hole she fled the apartment in terror; an apartment complex employee then discovered the tunnel, with Davis in it.

Davis was convicted of two counts of harassment, six counts of restraining order violations, and one count each of criminal trespass and attempted third-degree sexual assault. Amazingly, Davis was not charged under the state's stalking statute. This statute requires that the stalking behavior pose "a credible risk" to the victim; apparently the prosecutor's office believed the fact Davis had never made what the office considered a "verbal threat" to Jones precluded Davis from being charged with stalking. The judge gave Davis the maximum possible sentence for the relatively minor set of offenses of which he was convicted: nearly six years in jail.

Sixteen months later, Davis sought a sentence reduction. At the hearing, Davis's lawyer told the same judge who originally sentenced his client that Davis was "worth taking a chance on. Give him the benefit of the doubt . . . this obsessive behavior happened only once in 37 years." A psychologist then testified that he didn't believe Davis presented a danger to Jones or anyone else. "He's already understood the impact of his behavior and won't repeat his behavior," the psychologist testified. "He doesn't want contact with the victim." Another psychologist testified that Davis wasn't safe in the county jail. Because of the nature of his crime Davis had taken "a lot of abuse" there. After considering this testimony, the judge decided to place Davis on probation, on the condition that he leave the state, receive counseling, and live for a time under an officially monitored regimen.

Let us consider some of the features of our legal system illustrated by this case. First, we might note the absurdity of the claim that Davis's behavior never posed a "credible risk" to Jones. Here we see certain atavistic features of legal reasoning at work, with this reasoning taking place in a context of remarkably primitive psychological interpretation (i.e., if a stalker doesn't actually strike or explicitly threaten his victim, the stalker isn't posing a risk to the victim). Second, notice how our contemporary culture's belief in the value of therapeutic intervention devalues the core ethical ideal that a wrongdoer should suffer not merely for his own good, or for the protection of others, but because he deserves to suffer (i.e., modern therapeutic ideology tells us that once a wrongdoer is "cured" there can be no valid reason for punishing him). Third, note the lawyer's highly dubious assertion that this behavior happened "only once in 37 years" (for obvious reasons, stalking is one of the most underreported of crimes; indeed until quite recently it wasn't even recognized *as* a crime, leading one to wonder how it would be possible to determine this behavior had not happened before.)

Fourth, and of most relevance to the themes of this book, consider what in the context of this case the legal system treats as constituting "expert knowledge." The first psychologist's statement that Davis no longer poses a threat to the victim or anyone else can be nothing more than a sheer guess. This conclusion can't be more than a guess because numerous studies of the question have found there is simply no reliable method for predicting future dangerousness, other than to note that those persons who have exhibited dangerous tendencies in the past are more likely to be dangerous than those who have not.

The psychologist's claims that Davis has understood the impact of his behavior and therefore (?) won't repeat it, and that Davis doesn't want any contact with the victim are, if anything, even more questionable. How does the therapist know these things? Because Davis told him so? Persons in the grip of obsessive manias are notoriously good liars and routinely defeat the most elaborate attempts to measure their veracity.* Furthermore, the long-term prognosis for such persons is extremely poor: in time, they almost invariably relapse into some type of obsessional behavior. Add to this the fact that

---

*A circumstance that has served many litigators and law professors well.

Davis seems to have suffered considerable indignities while imprisoned—indignities that have likely produced deep feelings of victimization and fantasies of eventual revenge—and it becomes very difficult to give any credence at all to this "expert" testimony. Nevertheless the law in all its solemn idiocy must rely on *something*; and thus, on the basis of such therapeutic entrail-reading, it lets the wrongdoer go free.

Again, this sort of case illustrates how in contemporary public life legal and therapeutic modes of decision making can come to resemble frankly superstitious practices, whose invocation gives us a spurious sense of control over what remain insoluble mysteries of human behavior. Because in the context of a relentlessly rationalist culture the prospect of confronting the actual extent of our ignorance of the world terrifies us, we simply assume the rituals we perform to forestall that confrontation actually work.

Within the legal culture, the assumed efficacy of social practices such as criminal law and psychological counseling reflects this broader cultural faith in what is thought of as science. Indeed, as we have seen, the breakdown of the formalist conception of law as an autonomous discipline has given birth to the idea that, at least in "hard" cases, legal thinkers must extend the jurisdiction of law into the realm of what is thought of as "policy." Thus the modern law student is taught, either directly or by implication, that when the formal materials are indeterminate the outcome of a legal matter should be determined by the best policy; yet the student is also trained to believe that the content of this policy can and should be determined through the proper use of legal reasoning. Ideally, this instrumental use of reason is supposed to achieve a level of scientific rigor; hence the contemporary conception of law as a kind of "scientific policy making."

This gradual transformation of legal thought from a formal to a self-consciously instrumental practice has itself been enabled by the circumstance that, in the contemporary world, science has become the opium of the intellectuals. The reconceptualization of law as policy science is just one example of a more general trend. It is merely a prominent instance of how the cultural prestige of what is called the "scientific"—that is, the materialist—worldview has come to play a crucial role in producing a kind of rationalist addiction: an addiction to an intellectual narcotic that soothes the metaphysical anxieties of many a modern thinker. The weak magic of law draws what strength it has from the effects of a much stronger ideological intoxicant. And, if we are to fully understand our culture's abiding faith in its legal elixirs, we must turn our attention to this more powerful drug.

8

THE FUTURE OF AN ILLUSION

The materialist tradition is massive, complex, ubiquitous, and yet elusive. Its various elements—its attitude toward consciousness, its conception of scientific verification, its metaphysics and theory of knowledge— are all mutually supporting, so that when one part is challenged, the defenders can easily fall back on another part whose certainty is taken for granted ... [hence] the defenders do not feel it necessary to meet your actual arguments, because they know in advance you must be wrong. They know that the materialist tradition—which they often mistakenly call "science"—is on their side.

JOHN SEARLE, *The Rediscovery of the Mind*

I have great hopes that we shall learn in due time how to emotionalize and mythologise their science to such an extent that what is, in effect, a belief in us (though not under that name) will creep in while the human mind remains closed to belief in the Enemy.... If once we can produce our perfect work—the Materialist Magician, the man not using, but veritably worshiping, what he vaguely calls "Forces" while denying the existence of "Spirits"—then the end of the war will be in sight.

C. S. LEWIS, *The Screwtape Letters*

Here are two things you and I, if we are properly socialized members of our contemporary intellectual culture, are more or less required to believe.

1. The universe consists entirely of particles in fields of force. There are no such things as spirit or soul or karma or God, except to the extent those entities are projections of the human mind. The human mind itself is either: (a) an independent emergent property of otherwise mindless biological processes, or (b) can be reduced entirely to a nonmental account of those same processes.*

2. All matter is a product of mechanistic material processes, and all life is a product of mindless evolutionary processes. Therefore all teleological (mindful, design-based) accounts concerning the ultimate nature of the world are false.

These propositions are central to the creed of that modern variety of secular materialist rationalism that has become the unofficial religion of the American cultural and political elites (which is not to deny, of course, that there are dissenters from this view within those social classes. But the point is that such persons are very much dissenters from the orthodox position). As John Searle has put it, "This world view is not an option. It is not simply up for grabs along with a lot of competing world views." Searle claims that the problem isn't a failure to come up with a proof for the existence of God or an afterlife, but rather "that in our deepest reflections we cannot take such opinions seriously." He recalls giving a lecture in India where members of the audience assured him they themselves had existed in earlier lives, and comments, "Given what I know about the way the world works, I could not regard their views as serious candidates for truth."

Now what is most interesting about this assertion is the claim to know the way the world works. Searle's claim that "the universe consists entirely of extremely small physical phenomena that we . . . call particles" requires that he know the universe does not, for example, consist of a series of discrete mental events that in some necessary sense provide at least part and perhaps all of the ontological essence of what we call "physical" phenomena. But how could he know such a thing? As David Hume remarked, Bishop Berkeley's arguments that "to be is to be perceived" were thoroughly unan-

---

*These competing views are well represented by, respectively, John Searle's *The Rediscovery of the Mind*, and Daniel Dennett's *Consciousness Explained*.

swerable—although Hume also noted they remained, *within his (and our) culture*, thoroughly unconvincing. But *why* are such arguments unconvincing? Certainly not because "the facts" tell us otherwise. For the facts are always facts only within some metaphysical framework that itself is not amenable to further evidence (this is the point of Nietzsche's famous aphorism that there are no "facts," only interpretations). Within congenitally idealist cultures the notion that the perceived universe could somehow subsist autonomously from some mind's perception of it is just as patently absurd as the denial of this claim is to us. Thus despite his own perceptive criticisms of dogmatic materialism, Searle in the end simply assumes as a matter of deep cultural faith the truth of a fundamentally materialist interpretive framework; and indeed it is only from within that particular set of postulates that he can claim to know what he says he knows.*

In a similar vein, Daniel Dennett declares in his book *Darwin's Dangerous Idea* that "anyone who doubts that the variety of life on this planet was produced by a process of evolution is simply ignorant —inexcusably ignorant," and goes on to suggest the evidence for this process being random and mindless is so overwhelming that it is simply impossible, rationally speaking, to treat the deepest beliefs of almost all human beings in every other time and place with anything other than his own mixture of intellectual condescension, ethnocentric contempt, and a certain hygienic loathing. ("We just can't have forced female circumcision, and the second-class status of women in Roman Catholicism and Mormonism, to say nothing of their status in Islam.")

Dennett's writing in several ways typifies the sort of thinking found deep inside intellectually complacent orthodoxies. First, like many zealous advocates of a culture's most embedded conventions, his thought seems to inhabit an irony-free zone. Thus in the midst of anathematizing all other belief systems as irrational melanges of often dangerous nonsense he informs us he "think[s] that there [is]

---

*"The method of postulating what we want has many advantages. They are the same as the advantages of theft over honest toil." Bertrand Russell, *Introduction to Mathematical Philosophy*.

no force on this planet more dangerous to us all than ... fanaticism," and then proceeds to elaborate on this point by issuing a condemnation of all the world's major religions, "as well as countless smaller infections." "Is there" he asks the reader, "a conflict between science and religion here? There mostly certainly is." Of course there is also a striking similarity between so-called "scientific" and "religious" modes of thought here, although it's fairly obvious we shouldn't hold our collective breath waiting for the author to notice it.

Second, the last sixty pages of Dennett's book provide a wonderfully clear example of the intense cognitive dissonance that marks the orthodox contemporary view. For another key feature of that view is what might be called "meaning-laden nihilism." This is a sort of "Nietzsche lite," adopted by modern intellectuals who accept Nietzsche's most important claim ("God is dead"), but who are unable to accept the ethical consequences of that claim. The resulting cognitive dissonance allows Dennett to make statements such as "perhaps talk of rights *is* nonsense upon stilts, but *good* nonsense." It is "good only because it is on stilts, only because it happens to have the 'political' power to keep rising above [our questions]—not indefinitely, but usually 'high enough'—to reassert itself as a compelling—that is, conversation-stopping—'first principle.'"

Nietzsche—that most ruthlessly self-critical of thinkers—would have been sickened by this kind of thing. The idea, you see, is that even though we now believe unicorns are solely creatures of our imaginations, we are still habituated to a cultural practice in which we talk about unicorns as if they existed autonomously from our beliefs about them. This habit, however, is a "good" thing, because it produces "good" consequences. (Note how, given the underlying anti-teleological assumptions of the author's evolutionary materialism, the meaning of the term "good" must remain deeply mysterious.)* Along similar lines, Dennett admits that although accepting

---

*In other words: to the extent a theory of evolution is treated as an account of certain *biological processes*, that theory remains more or less amenable to scientific verification. When, however, it is treated as the key to some *anti-teleological metaphysic*, the metaphysical primacy of a mindless process of evolution more or less eliminates the possibility of discovering any objective basis for ideas of right and wrong, this nevertheless "is not an occasion for despair; we have the mind-tools we need to design and redesign ourselves, ever searching for better [?] solutions to the problems we create for ourselves and others."

Dennett's book illustrates some of the deeply dissonant beliefs intellectuals who cleave to the contemporary orthodoxy must accept. On the one hand the world is assumed to be a product of mindless processes that care nothing for human concerns, or for that matter anything else. Yet our vocabularies and indeed our very beings seem saturated by ways of talking that, given this axiomatic assumption, no longer make any sense. The dissonant intellectual then deals with this contradiction in much the same way a judge deals with the conclusory nature of a legal assertion: by failing to notice it.

Here, for example, is the well-known cosmologist Carl Sagan, on what he takes to be humanity's place in the universe:

> The Apollo pictures of the whole earth conveyed to the multitudes something well known to astronomers: On the scale of worlds—to say nothing of stars and galaxies—humans are inconsequential, a thin film of life on an obscure and solitary lump of rock and metal. . . . Our posturings, our imagined self-importance, the delusion that we have some privileged position in the Universe, are challenged by this point of pale light.

So inured are we to this way of talking that it is easy for us to overlook the flagrant incoherence of the interpretive metaphysics underlying this particular passage. It is of course true that if human beings are inconsequential—if it is indeed the case that the world is an obscure and solitary lump of rock—then we would in fact be deluded to think we have some privileged position in what Carl

"believing" in the doctrine of evolution becomes exactly as much a matter of faith as believing in the doctrine of the Virgin Birth—with which, by the way, it shares some interesting typological parallels.

Sagan calls "the Universe." But what the present confused state of our intellectual culture causes us to forget is just this: when they refer to humanity's actual metaphysical condition, comparative terms such as "inconsequential," "obscure," "solitary," and "privilege" can be understood as meaningful only *by reference to some transcendent—which is to say more than merely human—standard of evaluation.* In other words, if human beings are *truly* inconsequential, then something or someone must be consequential. If we are obscure, then some other entity is not. If we are solitary, then we are alone by comparison to those who have escaped cosmic isolation. And so forth. From a strictly materialist perspective, it is every bit as absurd to describe human beings as inconsequential as it is to declare them the center of the universe. Such an interpretive framework renders all comparative metaphysical judgments equally meaningless.

Daniel Dennett and Carl Sagan both continue to employ a thoroughly teleological vocabulary, and with it many of the implicit interpretive assumptions that must accompany the use of such a rhetoric. Yet both writers make arguments that claim to be grounded in those basic anti-teleological assumptions—materialist universe, mindless evolution—John Searle tells us we have no option but to accept, while seemingly remaining oblivious to the severe pragmatic contradictions created by the simultaneous employment of these two rationally irreconcilable ways of talking.

Now I am going to pose a highly inconvenient question. What *evidence* is there that this anti-teleological interpretation of the world is true? What evidence, that is, makes this view more plausible than every single one of the myriad teleological accounts of the nature of things that have flourished in every human culture? Here is the answer: there is none. John Searle, Daniel Dennett, Carl Sagan, and their countless epigoni that populate our little corner of this world quite simply *have faith* in their fundamental view of things.*

---

*A technical aside: Searle has made a number of amusing criticisms of the frankly bizarre views held by Dennett and many other contemporary philosophers of mind, whose attitude toward their subject is essentially that it doesn't exist (see the discussion of eliminative materialism, strong artificial intelligence, etc., in Searle's *The*

Surely this is an absurd statement. Surely science has proven . . . now what has science "proven," exactly? What, we might ask, have we learned about the ultimate questions—questions such as why is there something rather than nothing; has there always been something, or did something come of nothing and if so, how; is the world one thing or many, or does this question mean anything; do human beings have a special role in the world, and what might it be; what is the relation between the perceiver and the perceived; is mind part of matter or matter part of mind; what *are* "mind" and "matter"; what does it mean to say an action is right or wrong, and how do we tell the difference—what, again, have we learned about the answers to such questions that wasn't known by our ancestors? In a word: nothing. For all the technological achievements of science, and for all the predictive power it has given us over certain elements of our world, the scientific method—like every other method of inquiry and manner of thought—remains almost totally helpless when confronted with metaphysical questions the answers to which *we assume on faith* when we find ourselves committed to our fundamental worldviews.

What, after all, do we actually know? As Wittgenstein puts it, "If you do know that *'here is one hand,'* we'll grant you all the rest." But Wittgenstein's point is that you don't "know" even this, if by "know" is meant something more than "the psychological experience of certainty that is a product of the interpreter's unconscious reliance on the truth of various nonverifiable interpretive axioms." And even if we ignore the difficulty that all our supposed knowledge must be

---

Rediscovery of the Mind at pp. 5–26). It may be worth noting in this context that if we accept Searle's powerful arguments that consciousness is in some nontrivial sense ontologically distinct from nonconscious forms of matter, then Searle's assumption that mind is an emergent property of matter is surely no more plausible—and indeed possibly less so—than the assumption that matter is an emergent property of mind. (To put it in philosophical jargon: if you are a monist, favoring materialism over idealism can be at best an arbitrary choice.) The potentially devastating effect this latter point has for the materialist metaphysics to which both Searle and his philosophical opponents cling may well have some explanatory significance regarding *how and why* those opponents are capable of believing the otherwise incredible things about the nature of the human mind Searle so effectively criticizes them for believing.

grounded in unprovable assumptions, we must still confront the ver-
tiginous truth that, as Jorge Luis Borges puts it, "There is no classification of the universe that is not arbitrary and conjectural. The
reason," Borges reminds us, "is very simple: we do not know what
the universe is." The rationalist ethos of our time dismisses such
points as metaphysical quibbling, and proceeds on the assumption
that we *do* know what the universe is; indeed its priests are even now
assuring us that, save for a few details (which the laity is to understand are scheduled to be cleared up any day now), we are on the
verge of achieving a Final Theory of Everything: a kind of Re-
statement of the Real. But is such an ethos truly *scientific*?

Near the end of his life, Isaac Newton wrote this about the series
of revolutionary discoveries he had made:

> I do not know how I may appear to the world; but to myself I seem to
> have been only like a boy, playing on the seashore, and diverting
> myself, in now and then finding another pebble or prettier shell than
> ordinary, while the great ocean of truth lay all undiscovered before me.

This is the modesty of acknowledged genius, but no less valid for
that. What Newton understood was how, given the limitations of
space and time, and given the inevitably distorting effects our limited powers of perception and the particularity of our historical per-
spectives always generate, human knowledge can never be more
than a few grains of sand on that vast beach of all those things *we
know we do not know*. Beyond this lies the ocean of the invisible
unknown: of those things of which our ignorance is so complete that
we remain unaware of even the mere fact of that ignorance.

Yet consider how without exception the conventional wisdom of
every rationalist age has always been as follows: "After countless
centuries of ignorance and prejudice, of purblind superstition and
irrational reverence for the follies of the past, men have at long last
donned the mantle of reason and looked about them with eyes wide
open." And on doing so what have they discovered? Why, they have
found that within the span of one or two generations (theirs) almost
all the most profound questions that befuddled their ancestors

either have been or are about to be answered. Perhaps the most remarkable aspect of the eternally recurring belief that we are at the very brink of the final answer, and are thus approaching the apotheosis of reason itself, is that a key piece of evidence invariably adduced to illustrate the lamentable ignorance and folly under which our ancestors labored is that they believed precisely the same thing!

But the hubris that characterizes contemporary rationalist dogma is even more striking. Ever since the so-called Enlightenment, modern intellectuals have moved gradually from arguing for to accepting as self-evident what should be an extraordinarily counterintuitive claim. The claim is that in all previous cultures men and women have not only been *wrong* about the precise nature of the cosmic *telos*, but have been utterly deluded in believing there even *was* such a thing. In other words human beings are such weak-minded, fallible creatures that throughout recorded history their most profound beliefs about the nature of the world were not merely mistaken, but represented without exception various farragoes of contemptible, superstitious nonsense, having no relationship whatsoever to what we now know to be the case. What is most extraordinary about this claim is how it never includes any attempt to account for the unique —indeed, one might even call it providential—set of historical circumstances that has miraculously exempted our particular culture from the effects of what are otherwise apparently universal cognitive limitations. We are, it would seem, a chosen people.

Someone once remarked to T. S. Eliot that the difference between modern artists and the old masters was that "we know so much more than they did." "Yes," replied Eliot, "and they are what we know." And again, what *do* we know? Consider what we call "history." What would a true history of nothing but the brief moment it has taken me to write this sentence include? To even begin to imagine the richness of the billions of lives around us is to grasp how in some fraction of those lives a countless number of momentous events sprung into being in the course of that moment and then disappeared, without leaving us the slightest chance of undertaking a systematic or collective recovery of their essence. How many destinies were altered, how many long-nurtured dreams achieved their mark, or were broken beyond hope of redemption?

In that moment we can imagine a glass was crushed under a passionate foot in a Greek mountain village; a Russian civil servant threw away his career in an instant of brave protest; a novice entered for the first time the cool silence of a Zen monastery's garden; a poor Indian fisherman saw a glint of gold along the languid banks of an Amazonian tributary; a woman's tear glinted in the last rays of a tropical sun; another shovelful of dirt was tossed on a freshly dug grave; and from the trembling branch of elm, on which the last seven leaves of summer still clung, two crows cast themselves into somber and heavy-winged flight, somewhere in Nebraska. And of course all these things would themselves constitute nothing more than drops of water in that Heracletian river of potentially significant, historically irrecoverable human events.

We are told to learn from science. Let us do so. What are the teachings of such impeccable disciplines as quantum physics and chaos theory? If we take what the most rigorous modern learning proposes to heart, we will have to admit that any of these countless events, like the famous butterfly in Brazil, the fluttering of whose wings unleashes a hurricane two months later in New England, might constitute the key to understanding the subsequent workings of human history. Yet simply because they disappeared so quickly from our collective recollection, leaving behind little or no recoverable evidence of their presence in the world, we tell ourselves they were not "relevant" to a rational understanding of our destinies. Indeed, given the radical epistemological limitations under which we always labor, the credo of every rationalist age must be, "we *have faith* that what we do not know will not make shambles of all our supposed knowledge."

What we call "history" can be nothing but our weak conceptualization of a few mostly random fragments we have plucked out of the tiniest sliver of the past. We use such concepts to order the intolerable complexity of things into an apparent pattern, telling ourselves, absurdly enough, that something called "the Middle Ages" was succeeded by "the Renaissance." What an infinite array of precious, irretrievable knowledge is buried beneath those flimsy formulations. And how well the Talmud puts it when it says that with every man's death, a whole universe passes away. Reader, in the time it has taken your eyes to pass over this wordy and useless polemic thousands of individual worlds, with all their passions and their conquests, with their friendships, their ambitions, their tragedies, and their secret dreads, were annihilated without a trace, and passed far beyond the reach of our meager verbal formulae and impoverished categories of analysis. And all this, of course, is but the most infinitesimal fraction of the *true* history of those events that even now are happening all around us.

The priests of reason look for universal truth, for that which as they put it, "is true in all possible universes," although they have seen only one. Yet what, we might ask, do they know of the thousands of rituals, of cultures, of languages, of ways of being in the world, that have been utterly lost to what is called history? Of everything about the world ever known by human beings on what Carl Sagan considered an insignificant planet not one part in a billion billions is retained by the collective memory of men and women, let alone by any single human mind, however powerful its skills of reasoning might be. For all we know, some divinity perceives that infinitely reticulated web of what to us remains wholly obscure knowledge with the same intuitive clarity with which we grasp the shape of a triangle. What then would we make of what our secular priests call "reason"?

Were they there when Callimachus, who we are told handled marble as if it were bronze, fashioned a sculpture of translucent stone so delicate it stood but a single day? And where were they when the inconceivable mind of Michelangelo saw in a slab of Florentine marble the face of Moses burning like a living flame, as he brought down from the sacred mountain the words of the Law, held aloft in the hands of the outlaw? Can our secular priests even begin to grasp the sublimity of those Pascalian spaces, of those immense vistas of space and time by comparison to which our entire solar system is nothing more than a stone well, hidden in a corner of a field, beneath a ridge of hills that lie at the foot of a mountain range, whose most distant and inaccessible peaks divide the rushing waters of a vast continent? It may be that the entire history of the human race—of which, I repeat, we know almost nothing—is but an eyeblink of a galactic history of which we remain utterly ignorant. Sagan himself often speculated that there could well exist millions of inhabited worlds in our galaxy alone, complete with their unimaginable languages, their mythologies, their gods, their ceremonies, their systems of classification, and their ways of knowledge. Perhaps worlds hidden from us by the great stellar clouds of the Milky Way harbor crystalline forms of life that spend eons forming a single thought; or perhaps within such worlds entire civilizations subsist in the intermittent eddies of violent electromagnetic storms. Humanity will never know any of this. And yet even this incomprehensibly greater history might itself seem of little account, if it could somehow be compared to all that which in truth is past, or passing, or to come.

Frogs at the Bottom of the Well

William Butler Yeats's great poem "At Algeciras—a Meditation upon Death," ends with the following lines:

> Greater glory in the sun,
> An evening chill upon the air,
> Bid imagination run
> Much on the Great Questioner;
> What He can question, what if questioned I
> Can with a fitting confidence reply.

The dogmatic rationalist, the philosopher who can write sentences such as "I have learned that arguments, no matter how watertight, often fall on deaf ears," and "I am myself the author of arguments that I consider rigorous and unanswerable" (*Darwin's Dangerous Idea*, p. 12) has by contrast an almost unlimited faith in the powers of human ratiocination. The idea that human beings have the ability to make "watertight" and "unanswerable" claims about the nature of the world (as opposed to claims about the empty symbols they manipulate when they employ various types of tautological reasoning)* is a symptom of how the contemporary worship of analytical and supposedly scientific modes of thought can shade off into a type of dogmatic pseudo-religious belief, and eventually into the realm of a sort of intellectualized irrationalism.

The anthropologist Sir James Frazer ended his famous study *The Golden Bough* by comparing human thought to a fabric made of three threads: a black one representing magic, a red strand standing for religion, and a white thread symbolizing science. Writing at the dawn of the twentieth century Frazer shared his culture's deep faith in the power of reason, and in what was assumed to be the ineluctably linear progress of human thought. It is thus understandable Frazer believed it was historically destined that black should give way to red, and that the white thread would soon overwhelm both the others. We, who at the end of that century sit upon the unprecedented pile of corpses this same faith has helped wrought, have less excuse for cleaving so blindly to that particular illusion. For, as we should have learned by now, the colors of Frazer's fabric must always be blended more inextricably amid the labyrinthine paths of the human mind than a naive faith in the power of reason would allow.

"Frogs at the bottom of the well," goes the Chinese proverb, "see only part of the sky." We can be confident that in the language of such frogs the words for "well" and for "universe" are exact synonyms. And it also seems likely that, at the bottom of any particular well, frogs who question the classic definition of the universe ("a ubiquitous stone shaft") will be assured they are "simply ignorant— inexcusably ignorant" of this self-evident truth concerning the world's ultimate nature: a truth the power of amphibious reason has demonstrated conclusively every rational frog is required to acknowledge and accept.

---

*"So far as the laws of mathematics refer to reality, they are not certain. And so far as they are certain, they do not refer to reality." Albert Einstein, *Geometry and Experience*.

9

THE BANALITY OF GOODNESS

Science, thanks to its links with observation, retains some title to a correspondence theory of truth. But a coherence theory is evidently the lot of ethics.

WILLARD VON ORMAN QUINE, *Theories and Things*

The best lack all conviction, while the worst
Are full of passionate intensity.

YEATS, "The Second Coming"

"Napalming babies," observed Arthur Leff, "is bad." This I am willing to grant; although as Richard Posner points out in his inimitably relentless fashion, even that sort of moral statement needs to be qualified by its particular context (just or unjust war; unavoidable consequence of battle or negligent infliction of civilian casualties, etc.). The essay in which Leff made this observation, "Unspeakable Ethics, Unnatural Law," makes a stark case for the depth of the crisis modernity faces in regard to the evaluation of ethical and moral questions. Nietzsche sums up that crisis in a single sentence: "Now suppose that belief in God has vanished: the question presents itself anew: 'who speaks?'" Let us pursue the answer to this question in the particular context of legal argument and judicial decision making.

Compare the statements "I believe the Earth revolves around the Sun" and "I believe Häagen-Dazs ice cream tastes better than Ben & Jerry's." In our culture the first statement will be generally understood as a claim about the objective nature of the world, while the second will be interpreted as a statement about subjective prefer- ence. In other words, the belief in a heliocentric solar system is understood to be a belief about the way things are, independent of any human belief or desire. By contrast, the claim about the superi- ority of Häagen-Dazs ice cream is taken to be *nothing other than* a claim about the content of certain human desires and beliefs. Thus the statement "for me the Earth goes around the Sun, but for you the Sun may well revolve around the Earth" would be treated as being just as absurd as the claim that the taste of Häagen-Dazs is *objectively* superior to that of Ben & Jerry's, independent of whatever opinions people might hold regarding the latter question.

In the 1930s the logical positivist movement in philosophy came up with some useful terms for sorting these different types of truth claims out from each other. The logical positivists claimed that "true" statements were either true by definition (e.g., logical and mathematical statements), or were empirically verifiable claims about the objective facts of some matter ("the Earth revolves around the Sun"). On the other hand, statements about personal prefer- ences ("Häagen-Dazs tastes better than Ben & Jerry's") were catego- rized as "emotive." Such statements were either treated as examples of a kind of degraded "subjective truth," or indeed in the more rig- orous versions of the logical positivist creed were considered to be, strictly speaking, meaningless.

Now consider the statement "Abortion is murder." Obviously this claim can, like any other, be interpreted as a logical proposition; but just as obviously nothing of ethical importance turns on such a triv- ial interpretation of its meaning. Can it be understood as an empiri- cal claim? The logical positivists thought that it couldn't. Being believers in good standing in the church of anti-teleological materi- alism (the universe is made up of nothing but particles; life is a prod- uct of mindless evolutionary processes, etc.) they could not imagine what *fact of the matter* would make such a statement empirically true. Hence they dismissed all ethical claims as emotive statements, illus- trating the subjective beliefs and preferences of those who made them, but nothing more.

It soon became clear that, despite its formal elegance, logical positivism was at the least a very inadequate model for understanding the psychology of human belief. For nothing is more obvious than that when people make statements such as "Abortion is murder" they do not believe they are merely signaling their personal preferences. Hardly anyone, that is, believes the claim "Napalming babies is bad" is equivalent to saying "Coke tastes better than Pepsi." Still, the logical positivists made a disturbing point: if ethical assertions cannot to be reduced to either trivial definitional claims, or examples of wholly subjective human beliefs, what sorts of claims do such assertions involve? Or, as Nietzsche put it, "Who speaks?"

Nietzsche's formulation of the issue reminds us that, within the context of a teleological worldview, this question has an answer. If the world is so constituted that there really is such a thing as objective human virtue—"objective" precisely because that virtue does not merely reflect human beliefs, but actually corresponds with the demands of some metaphysical *telos*, or ultimate design and purpose of the world—then it is by reference to the nature and content of this design that we can make true ethical claims. Teleological accounts of what constitutes the good present their own problems, of course (what is the nature and content of the world's design; how can we discover it, etc.); but at least they as a logical matter succeed in separating out moral claims from mere assertions of subjective belief and preference. Thus when Nietzsche speaks of belief in God vanishing, he isn't merely speaking of belief in the personal Christian God, or indeed of belief in any deity in particular. He is speaking of the ethical consequences that flow from the much broader phenomenon of the triumph of the materialist, anti-teleological faith. Within *that* set of assumptions about the nature of the world (and, as I argued in the previous chapter, they must be *assumptions*—having faith in not having faith being just as much a species of ungrounded metaphysical belief as any other) it becomes difficult to see why the harshest judgments of the logical positivists were not correct. For if you deny any transcendent metaphysical significance to your ethical statements, and yet at the same time insist they are not merely culturally sanctioned subjective beliefs,* then what exactly is the *meaning* of such statements? Just what sort of fact is being asserted here?

The characteristic crisis of ethical interpretation among modern intellectuals is thus a product of the combination of an anti-teleological worldview with vocabularies and modes of thought that, given this view, no longer make any sense. Again, what we see so often in contemporary ethical debate is analogous to the continuation of passionate arguments concerning the biology of the unicorn when all belief in the unicorn as an actual biological entity has vanished. Various strategies are then employed to deal with this incoherent interpretive situation. As we have seen, one of the most common is to fail to grasp the contradictory nature of the claims. Thus Daniel Dennett is committed to a worldview in which the different levels of political participation granted women in various human cultures have exactly the same metaphysical significance as the different levels of status granted to females in the hierarchies of any other species (i.e., these differences must be understood at bottom as more or less "successful" evolutionary adaptations to local conditions on the part of the species in question), and yet he still feels himself impelled to proclaim that "we just can't have ... the second-class status of women in Roman Catholicism ..." etc., etc. Given the nihilistic metaphysics that underlie what he calls "Darwin's dangerous idea," one might want to ask just who *is* this "we," as well as why it is that "we" can't have this. Because the prac-

---

*Despite the claims of cultural relativists to the contrary, the fact that everyone might agree with an ethical assertion can make no difference to its metaphysical status as truth. In other words, to assert "Everyone thinks chocolate tastes good" isn't to assert the same *sort* of claim about human belief's relation to the actual nature of the world as to assert "Everyone thinks incest is wrong," even if, as a matter of social fact within a particular culture, both claims happen to be true. In the first case, the cultural relativist's perspective is perfectly adequate: the belief in the good taste of chocolate is simply *identical* with that which is asserted to be the case. Yet it is difficult to imagine what moral claims would even mean if in their case human belief and ethical truth were understood to be identical in this same radically subjectivized, observer-relative way.

tices of certain cultures offend the moral sensibilities of Daniel Dennett? They obviously don't offend the moral sensibilities of others; and after all there simply can be no *scientific* basis for objecting to those practices. What we call "science" is limited to the business of providing accurate physical descriptions, rather than normative metaphysical objections. That, too, is part of Darwin's dangerous idea.

Another strategy, much favored by analytical philosophers, is what might be called the "magic word" gambit. The idea here is that when one is confronted with an inexplicable phenomenon, one can give the impression of knowledge by inventing a word that appears to redescribe usefully this otherwise inexplicable state of affairs. Hence when moral philosophers of a certain stripe are confronted with the fact that, in the contemporary world, statements of value seem not to involve empirical claims, but nevertheless still seem irreducible to mere tautologies or statements of preference, they will begin to burble enthusiastically about ethical "supervenience," or about moral "modalities" of argument. On closer examination these terms will be found to play the same role in contemporary moral argument that the invocation of the "taboo" plays among certain preindustrial peoples. Ethnographers have discovered that among such peoples the status of the taboo often can't be explained by reference to any consequences said to follow from its breach (i.e., sickness, bad luck), or by any more overtly teleological explanation as to why the taboo is forbidden (such as the gods prohibiting it). The activity is simply deemed "taboo." In such societies the belief in the forbidden nature of the taboo thus appears to be an example of frank irrationalism. Yet the assumption that the deployment of theoretical terminology equals the possession of practical knowledge remains so deeply embedded in the human mind that it is perfectly possible for both complex cultural practices and erudite scholarly literatures to be erected around the invocation of such apparently empty signifiers.

Still another approach is illustrated in the following passage from an essay by the well-known professor of classics and (recently) law, Martha Nussbaum.

As Nietzsche showed, it is only to someone whose faith in his own human capacities has been eroded by the teachings of an otherworldly faith that the news of the death of God brings nihilism and the abandonment of evaluation and selection. The failure of these thinkers to commit themselves to sorting out our human and historical practices of choice and selection, the insistence that we could have good normative arguments only if they came from heaven—all this betrays a shame before the human. On the other hand, if we really think of the hope of a transcendent ground for value as uninteresting or irrelevant to human ethics, as we should, then the news of its collapse will not change the way we think and act. It will just let us get on with *the business of reasoning* in which we are already engaged. [emphasis added]

One of the more intrepid things an academic reader of philosophy can do is to cite Nietzsche in support of a normative proposition regarding the role of reason in the maintenance of moral discourse. Indeed, it is somewhat startling to juxtapose Professor Nussbaum's observations with a few of Nietzsche's own words:

When one finds it necessary to turn *reason* into a tyrant, as Socrates did, the danger cannot be slight that something else will play the tyrant. Rationality was then hit upon as the savior; neither Socrates nor his "patients" had any choice about being rational: it was *de rigeur*, it was their last resort. The fanaticism with which all Greek reflection throws itself upon rationality betrays a desperate situation; there was danger, there was but one choice: either to perish or—to be *absurdly rational*.

To quote the author of *The Antichrist* and *Twilight of the Idols* for the proposition that accepting the death of God does not in fact herald the arrival of nihilism in Western thought; and, even more remarkably, to imagine that what Nietzsche called "the revaluation of all values" entails nothing more than "get[ting] on with the business of reasoning in which we are already engaged"—what are these claims but evidence of that very *decadence of reason* of which Nietzsche warned? It is no exaggeration to say these assertions invoke nothing less than the precise negation of Nietzsche's most distinctive and characteristic ideas. Such talk betrays, to echo the Nietzschean intonations of Professor Nussbaum, a shame before the *inhuman*: before the metaphysical void that Nietzsche, at least, had the courage to acknowledge made nonsense of the moral chimeras at the center of all those "human and historical practices of [ethical] choice and selection" Professor Nussbaum urges us to continue pursuing more or less exactly as before.

For what, in the end, is this "business of reasoning" supposed to be reasoning *about*? About what you or I, or for that matter Professor Nussbaum, believe are truly ethical choices? Such beliefs cannot be interpreted as the products of a rational process aimed at determining what is *actually* good, unless our arguments about the good refer to something other than our respective beliefs about the good. What then are we to make of the fact so many contemporary academics deny that the total *subjectivization* of ethical argument— the reduction of the good to *beliefs* about the good, whether these beliefs be those of individuals, communities, or entire cultures— must of necessity rob the practice of ethical argument of most of its meaning and purpose? Is this fact merely another sign of the solipsistic decadence that marks much of our moral and political discourse? Or is it, perhaps, an illustration of what can only be understood as a collective loss of cultural and intellectual nerve?

This isn't the place for a disquisition regarding the deadly effects of academic pedantry on the interpretation of so much of what were, before the academic disciplinarians got their hands on them, original and arresting ideas. Yet still—if I might be permitted a prayer to whatever form of transcendence has been granted us, even if it should turn out to be nothing more than the superannuated and deficient divinity of a degraded Gnostic universe—oh Divine Presence, if you should ever turn your eternal gaze in our miserable direction, *please spare us from the "Nietzsche" of the professors!* Nietzsche, who above all else was the father of radically heterodox and truly dangerous countercultural ideas, has been domesticated into a darling of the soporific university seminar: into a purveyor of prudential Aristotelian virtue, of liberal democratic "values" and—*mirabile dictu*—of the ideally neat, acontextually "objective," and intellectually arid conceptual categories of Anglo-American analytical philosophy. No form of incomprehension is worse than that of the learned.

Abortion and the Politics of Reason

Moral debate in our public culture is at present in a state of almost total confusion. With the collapse of any generally accepted teleological account of what is entailed in the praise or condemnation of morally significant human choices, we no longer have a widely shared sense of what it even means to call such choices "right" or "wrong." Needless to say, this state of affairs poses significant problems for law. Law requires bringing the violence of the state to bear on those who make certain moral choices, and using that same power to protect the freedom of others to choose differently. A thin formalist or positivist conception of law thus requires us to admit we are deploying state power without any justification beyond that of pointing out a particular deployment is required by the extant legal rules. (Example: We imprisoned Jones for five years because the legislature determined that those who sell ten pounds of marijuana should be imprisoned for five years.)

This situation makes legal actors unhappy. For while advocates or judges may sometimes be able to rationalize their role in the respective punishment and legitimation of various moral choices by telling themselves they are only following the rules, all but the most simpleminded realize both that the rules justify nothing in themselves, and that in any case many significant legal decisions are not in any meaningful sense impelled by those rules. Given their professional obligations, legal academics are even more acutely aware of these uncomfortable facts. The moral and psychological inadequacy of formalist justification thus gives rise to the rationalist urge: to the desire to find compelling reasons for adopting this rule rather than that one. Let us trace out some of the consequences of indulging that urge in a characteristically difficult social and legal context.

Arguments about the morality of abortion are of course classic illustrations of conflicts between deeply held, fundamentally irreconcilable views. These conflicts are structured around what in our culture are two points of almost unanimous agreement: the belief that infanticide is murder, and that the choice to have or not to have children should remain unregulated by the state. The moral status of the fetus between conception and birth then becomes a crucial question for the ethical and political analysis of the issue. It should be unnecessary to add that this is the sort of question that can't be answered empirically, as beliefs concerning what constitutes "personhood" are at bottom metaphysical acts of faith, and hence remain unamenable to empirical proof or refutation.

This question can be phrased in bivalent (i.e., when does the fetus become a person?) or multivalent terms (i.e., at what stages of development does the fetus have which attributes of personhood?). A separate set of questions revolve around what moral limits and obligations are imposed on others by the varieties of personhood attributed to the fetus. Yet another group of questions involve what legal rules should govern our moral conclusions, whatever those may be.

Within these sets of considerations, an enormous number of conclusions can be drawn that are neither susceptible to proof, nor subject to refutation. Besides the most obvious positions—the fetus is or is not a person at point X and hence abortion is or is not immoral, and should or should not be illegal at that same point—there are almost limitless possible variations: the fetus is a person, and abortion is immoral, but it should not be prohibited because such prohibitions are unenforceable and do more harm than good; the fetus is in some ways like a person, but not enough for considerations of the morality of abortion to overcome the importance of individual moral choice; the fetus is only a little like a person, but abortion is therefore deeply wrong and should be outlawed, if only to symbolize our respect for all human life; the fetus is somewhat of a person, and thus has certain legal rights, but abortion in cases of rape and incest is a type of justifiable homicide—and so on and so on.*

---

*Note how ideologically driven arguments for a particular moral or legal view must deny the potential complexity of other views, if those who make such arguments are to claim persons who disagree with the proffered view are making rationally inconsistent claims. For a full critique of this rhetorical strategy in the context of arguments about abortion and reason, see Steven D. Smith, *The Constitution and the Pride of Reason*.

Arguments about abortion thus take place within a moral, social, and legal equilibrium zone. Again, within such a zone powerful competing considerations can be adduced for holding a variety of views. Furthermore such considerations can't be refuted without recourse to some axiomatic ground of argument that others do not accept and that, precisely because it *is* axiomatic, cannot be argued for rationally. Such disputes must end, if at all, in some act of arational assertion, and will have to be resolved accordingly.

The rationalist urge to deny this is part of rationalism's denial of what the philosopher Miguel de Unamuno called "the tragic sense of life." The idea that important values may be irreconcilably at odds with each other, and that the choice between them cannot be adjudicated by reason, is not dependent on accepting moral relativism; it merely requires we acknowledge that, as Isaiah Berlin puts it, "The [legitimate] values of one culture may be incompatible with those of another," and that we may find the same incompatibility within "one culture or group or in a single human being at different times." Berlin points out that such a "notion of a plurality of values not structured hierarchically" does not entail relativism, but it does entail "the permanent possibility of inescapable conflict between values."

The acceptance of intractable ethical pluralism and its potentially tragic implications must always be in great practical tension with what Robert Cover called the "jurispathic" character of legal decision making: faced with "the luxuriant growth of a hundred legal traditions, [judges] assert that *this one* is law and destroy or try to destroy all the rest." The weapon of choice in such jurispathic operations is often called "the law," or "the Constitution," or even "reason" itself. For example, in the course of an acknowledgment, rare within the legal academic literature, of the limits of reason in moral and legal decision making Professor Robin West points out that "reason will not account for, or in the end meaningfully challenge, our rock-bottom moral beliefs, and [Cass] Sunstein is simply wrong to think otherwise." West thus concludes correctly that on issues such as abortion "reason alone is not going to compel agreement."

At this point one might expect Professor West to, figuratively speaking, shrug her shoulders and move on. But that would leave the legal academic with nothing useful to contribute to the resolution of this particular legal debate; hence *ex hypothesi*, there must still be more to say. West thus goes on to argue that to function well our reason must be supplemented with an emotional, experiential component of knowledge. "If we are really aiming for genuine consensus," she says, "then the experiential gaps [in our various lives] must be bridged."

She then gives the following example. Many years ago, she saw a picture that has haunted her ever since. It was of a naked young woman who appeared to be sleeping peacefully, but who in fact had died after undergoing an illegal abortion. When she first saw this picture she was "filled with sadness and then with an overpowering feeling of identity." She relates that every year "at least one [law] student, usually a man, tells me that [this or some similar representation] changed his mind on abortion." The point is "that moral convictions are changed experientially or empathically, not through argument." West emphasizes she is "not advocating illogic or irrationality. What I am seeking to highlight is that injustice must be *shown*, not asserted. . . . Reason alone simply will not move us—but experience, empathy, and reflection might."

There is much to admire in this argument. As a description of the psychology of fundamental moral belief it is both more accurate and infinitely more attractive than the intellectual hubris of arguments that claim to demonstrate that reason either impels one to accept a particular moral view or, as in the case of the omniscient Professor Dworkin, requires the acolyte to accept that he *already* believes in the particular moral code the evangelist of reason brings unto the nations.* Still, what is missing here is any acknowledgment of the other side of the question. This omission seems all the more surprising when one considers that a crucial element of pro-life activism has been to undertake precisely the sorts of emotive and experiential

---

*See, for example, Dworkin's book *Life's Dominion*, which argues that opponents of abortion would not be against the practice if they truly understood their own moral beliefs.

consciousness-raising tasks that West advocates. Opponents of legalized abortion try to build that elusive "genuine consensus" on the issue by confronting the ambivalent with, for example, pictures of aborted fetuses that have been hacked to pieces in a procedure difficult to distinguish visually from simple infanticide. They also employ the narratives of self-proclaimed victims of abortion, women who relate how they carry burdens of almost intolerable guilt from having "killed their babies" as a consequence of the availability of legal abortion. Are these pictures and these stories somehow less legitimate, less compelling, than the pictures and stories employed by pro-choice advocates? Do they fail in the task of illustrating how "injustice must be *shown*"?

Obviously West believes they do. But this belief is no more defensible or, more to the point, transmissible to those who disagree with it than are the rationalist arguments she rightly chides Cass Sunstein for treating as more dispositive than *they* are. The experiential and emotive side of the abortion question is just as ineluctably tangled as its rationalist and axiomatic cousin. Indeed if it were not, then the reasons given for supporting a particular position on the question would convince practically everyone, even though those reasons themselves could not as a rational matter resolve the issue; or by contrast such reasons would convince no one at all, no matter how logically impeccable and rationally consistent they might be. After all, it is possible to make a perfectly coherent and rational argument for infanticide; and indeed many cultures have never considered that practice to be morally problematic. The irrelevance of this logical and historical fact to the American debate about abortion tells us much about the limits of reason; but it also indicates that the same *practical* limitations extend to those emotive factors that, as West points out, always undergird our most profound moral and political beliefs.

Legal Reasoning as Mental Illness

As I write these words, the Supreme Court has just announced that it will review two federal court decisions that found a constitutional right to physician-assisted suicide, and hence invalidated state legis-lation forbidding that practice. Once more the votaries of what is called constitutional law are thrusting themselves into the midst of an excruciatingly difficult public ethical debate, in order that they may tell us yet again what "the Constitution" requires Americans to believe concerning a matter of fundamental moral controversy. Of particular interest in this regard is the decision in *Quill v. Vacco*, in which a federal appeals court found that a New York state law penal-izing assisted suicide was not "rationally related to a legitimate state interest."

Physician-assisted suicide is yet another issue that lies squarely in the middle of a moral, social, and legal equilibrium zone. That zone was as a formal matter bounded by on the one side the legal right, now recognized in every American jurisdiction, of mentally compe-tent adults to refuse medical treatment and on the other, what was the almost equally universal prohibition forbidding persons from assisting another's suicide attempt.

Obviously the right to refuse medical treatment and the prohibi-tion on assisted suicide represent attempts to accommodate power-fully conflicting ethical and practical concerns. A strong cultural commitment to individual autonomy supports the view that seri-ously ill people should be allowed to end their lives as they see fit, without being subjected to unwanted and perhaps futile medical treatment. Indeed it has been estimated that 70 percent of the deaths that take place in hospitals and nursing homes are a direct product of the cessation of medical intervention. With nearly two-thirds of this society's vast medical care costs already being incurred within the last six months of people's lives, a requirement that heroic measures always be undertaken without regard to the wishes of the patient would quickly bankrupt the health care system. Thus in this instance the cultural commitment to individual choice dovetails nicely with frankly pragmatic fiscal concerns.

But this very coalescence of ideological commitment and eco-nomic interest is also, of course, a major reason why there are pow-erful arguments in favor of limiting our legal right to "choose" to kill ourselves. After all in a society in which suicide is a culturally and legally sanctioned choice, it will soon become obvious that it is very much in the interests of various parties to ensure that certain classes of persons understand how important it is they make that particular choice. Already, as the philosopher and bioethicist John Arras points out, physicians fail routinely to "diagnose and treat reversible clinical depression, especially in the elderly population." Arras further notes that nearly 40 million Americans lack decent primary medical care; that most physicians suffer from "an appalling lack of training in palliative care"; and that significant discrimination in the delivery of pain control and other medical treatment takes place on the basis of race and economic status. Furthermore, the sanguine assumption that abuses of a system of physician-assisted suicide or voluntary euthanasia can be regulated out of existence is not supported by comparative inquiry. The Dutch experience with legalized euthanasia suggests that in the Netherlands, despite copious regulations designed to avoid such things, several hundred patients are euthanized every year who did not actually consent to being killed.

Laws against physician-assisted suicide are in part attempts to protect society's most vulnerable members from those who wish to relieve society of the burden of that membership. As Professor Yale Kamisar puts it, the line drawn by the American legal system "between 'letting die' and actively intervening to bring about death represents a cultural and pragmatic compromise between the desire to let seriously ill people carry out their wishes to end it all and the felt need to protect the weak and vulnerable."

Faced with this welter of delicate considerations, the appeals court in *Quill v. Vacco* could, for reasons having to do with the peculiar institution of judge-created constitutional law doctrine, overturn the balance struck between them by the New York legislature only if it found either a "fundamental constitutional right" to assisted suicide, or if it determined that this law was not "rationally related to a legitimate state interest." After acknowledging a right to physician-assisted suicide "finds no cognizable basis in the Constitution's language or design" (a circumstance, by the way, that didn't keep the judges in the other case currently before the Supreme Court from finding such a right), the court noted that the New York law "does not treat equally all competent persons who are in the final stages of fatal illness and wish to hasten their deaths," and that in its view "the distinctions made by New York law with regard to such persons do not further any legitimate state purpose." It summed up its argument in the following passage:

> What business is it of the state to require the continuation of agony when the result is imminent and inevitable? What concern prompts the state to interfere with a mentally competent patient's [quoting *Planned Parenthood v. Casey*] 'right to define [his] own concept of existence, of meaning, of the universe, and of the mystery of human life,' when the patient seeks to have drugs prescribed to end life during the final stages of a terminal illness? The greatly reduced interest of the state in preserving life compels the answer to these questions: 'None.'"

Let us hope it is necessary to first be transformed into what Joseph Stalin referred to in another context as "a special breed of person" before one becomes capable of uttering such things in the name of what "the Constitution requires." Let us hope, that is, that this passage is a product of a lifetime of indulging in legal reasoning, and not a representative of its author's unindoctrinated cognitive abilities. For here are just a few of the considerations the author of this encomium to bureaucratized death overlooks or ignores.

First, the claim that no rational distinction can be drawn between the right to refuse medical treatment and the right to physician-assisted suicide is true only in a rationally trivial sense. It is true in the sense that no *compelling* distinction can be drawn between the two rights; but of course, when rational analysis is taking place within an equilibrium zone, no compelling distinction can *ever* be drawn between different positions.

In claiming that no such rational distinction can be drawn, the *Quill* court took advantage of an unavoidable logical and practical difficulty that besets any exercise in analytic line-drawing. All such line-drawing is vulnerable to a logical paradox that the ancient Greeks named a "sorites problem." A sorites problem arises in any logical context of the form "If A, then B; if B, then C; if C, ... if Y, then Z" so that the first term implies the last: if A, then Z. The philosopher Zeno formulated it thus: Suppose a heap of sand is comprised of n grains. Remove a grain. Is it still a heap? Yes. Remove another grain. Is it still a heap? . . . and so on. The point of the problem is that we can't describe accurately the transition from heap to not-heap because the analytic boundary between these concepts is fuzzy, rather than sharply defined.

Within moral, social, and hence legal equilibrium zones this problem is, as both a logical and practical matter, endemic. Almost everyone in this culture believes competent adults should be able to refuse medical treatment. Almost no one believes that involuntary euthanasia is morally acceptable. Between those relatively sharp lines come a whole series of fuzzy distinctions. Should competent adults be able to refuse food and water? Should terminally ill patients be able to obtain fatal doses of self-administered drugs? Should physicians be able to administer such drugs to willing patients? Should such measures be made available to those who are not terminally ill? How far should we go in "implying" the desires we believe incompetent patients would have if they were still competent? And so on.

Note that according to *Quill v. Vacco* a physician in New York who hands a terminally ill patient a fatal dose of morphine is vindicating the patient's constitutional rights; but if the physician injects a physically incapacitated patient with a fatal dose of the same drug in response to the patient's desperate pleas that he wants to die, the physician has committed a serious felony. How "rational" is *that* distinction? Indeed if we were to take the court's definition of what rational distinctions entail seriously, penalizing a driver for going sixty-six miles per hour on the interstate would have to be considered unconstitutional, as it is obviously impossible to demonstrate that it is "rationally related to a legitimate state interest" for the state to enforce a speed limit of sixty-five rather than sixty-six miles per hour—if, that is, we ignore the eminently rational need to draw some kind of line in the first place.

Within a legal equilibrium zone there will never be compelling reasons for drawing the analytic line at point l rather than at point m or point n; but of course there will also never be compelling reasons for drawing it at point *n* rather than point *m* or *l*. Thus nothing is easier—or more analytically trivial—than for a court to point out that there is no rationally compelling reason for distinguishing between two positions within such an equilibrium zone. And yet there will always be plenty of *rationally defensible* reasons—though not rationally compelling ones—for distinguishing between any of these various positions.

In the case of laws prohibiting physician-assisted suicide it is easy to point to all sorts of reasons why we might draw a line prohibiting physicians from helping their patients to kill themselves. Here are just a few: because terminally ill patients are often in situations of great pain and chronic depression, where the concept of informed consent becomes highly problematic; because determining what the phrase "terminal illness" does or should encompass is a much more difficult task than the neat conceptual categories employed in legal argument would have us believe; because once we sanction physician-assisted suicide it will become difficult or impossible to prohibit active euthanasia; because such "rights" will be used to pressure the elderly, poor people, ethnic minorities, the handicapped, and other marginalized persons to kill themselves; and because with the loosening of formal restrictions some doctors will be more likely to, as in the Netherlands, practice informal nonvoluntary euthanasia. (These reasons do not even touch on what may be the most powerful argument against the practice, which is that most of the major Western religious and philosophical traditions have considered suicide to be deeply wrong. Of course it merely begs the question to claim that making such moral judgments is none of the state's business.)

The *Quill* court responds to some of these concerns in a manner that once again illustrates the disabling effect the need to engage in the rationalization of legal decisions can have on the ability to undertake usefully rational analyses of difficult issues. Thus the court asserts "the state of New York may establish rules and procedures to assure that all choices are free of [coercive] pressures," and that "with respect to the protection of minorities, the poor and the non-mentally handicapped, it suffices [!] to say that these classes of persons are entitled to treatment equal to that afforded to all those who now may hasten death by means of life-support withdrawal." Of course the first point simply ignores the fact that the state of New York has *already* established what it sees as an appropriate regime of rules and procedures to assure that seriously ill persons are not coerced into suicide, in the form of the very laws the court is invalidating. And what can possibly be the point of asserting that marginalized persons "are entitled to equal treatment?" After all, the special concern about the possible coercion of members of otherwise vulnerable groups obviously has nothing to do with the *formal* legal rights those groups already enjoy.

The almost surreal irrelevance of these responses can be interpreted as a product of what are at bottom various delusional patterns of thought concerning both the efficacy and the justificatory force of legal regulations. We might conclude that legal actors who actually believe the sorts of claims made by the court in the *Quill* case are in the grip of a professional deformation that has many of the qualities of a mental illness. Yet the presence of this cognitive pathology isn't in itself evidence that there is something "wrong" with such legal thinkers. Indeed, as I have argued, properly socialized lawyers are in a sense *required* to inhabit a cognitive universe that features profoundly untenable assumptions concerning the relationship between legal imperatives and the social reality these imperatives are attempting to regulate. Such legal actors are thus to some extent impelled to adopt irrational beliefs regarding legal reason's power to determine rationally what those imperatives should be.

Cases such as this also illustrate the special role the U.S. Constitution plays in the maintenance of a species of mystifying obscurantism at the base of American law. (I should emphasize that this isn't necessarily a criticism. It is only from a rationalist perspective that mystification and obscurantism are *necessarily* bad things.) When the Supreme Court rules on the question of assisted suicide, few lay observers will ever be aware that the law supposedly compelling whatever result it reaches will be one or another clause of a sentence reading "nor shall any State deprive any person of life, liberty, or property, without due process of law; nor deny to any person within its jurisdiction the equal protection of the laws."* This sentence, like so many other clauses of the Constitution, is read today as if it were some grand evocation of highly abstract moral and political principles, when in fact as a matter of history such clauses were without exception relatively modest responses to what at the time were understood to be quite local and particularized disputes.

But history is of little relevance to the interpretation of a fetishized cultural artifact. The Constitution has become to many members of a certain American social class what the prophecies of Nostradamus represent to those of another: an ideally vague set of oracular-sounding propositions, whose very vagueness comfort the devotee with a sense that the correct interpretation of an essentially magical text will provide insight into mysteries that would otherwise remain unknowable and obscure.

The Banality of Goodness

Why *is* napalming babies "bad?" Given the current state of our intellectual culture, we can no longer be sure what this question even means, let alone how to answer it. Thus if we turn to courts for answers to questions of the most profound moral resonance, perhaps we do so in part because we no longer know how to talk about such things without resorting to the analytic circularities and rhetorical sophistries of legal reasoning. Yet anyone who believes that thinking very carefully about matters of deep moral disagree-

---

*Despite various pleas that this was too important an issue to be decided democratically (see, e.g., the self-styled "Philosopher's Brief" filed by Ronald Dworkin, et al.) the Supreme Court found no constitutional right to physician-assisted suicide. Commentators generally praised the Court for not imposing its views on the democratic process. Two days earlier, many of the same commentators had been equally effusive in their praise when the Court struck down a federal statute (the Religious Freedom Restoration Act) that had passed both Houses of Congress with a total of three dissenting votes. It is indeed unfortunate that, on this latter occasion, our elected representatives proved almost unanimously incapable of understanding "what the Constitution requires."

ment will make those matters usefully amenable to the powers of human reason needs to think about that belief some more.

But this conclusion leaves us faced with a considerable mystery. It remains an article of faith in both legal and academic circles that indulging in extensive reasoning about such matters makes sense: indeed the more extensive, the better. A particularly interesting illustration of this belief is provided by Judge Guido Calabresi's concurrence in the *Quill* decision.

Judge Calabresi is in his own right an unusually distinguished legal scholar, so it comes as no surprise that his concurrence is, as an intellectual matter, vastly more impressive than the majority's almost comically weak opinion. Judge Calabresi concurs with the majority's conclusion that, on the record before the court, the New York statutes prohibiting physician-assisted suicide are unconstitutional. But he admits that the underlying ethical and social issues are "*of extreme difficulty*" (his emphasis). He alludes to Margaret Mead's troubling observation that we should beware giving those who have the power to heal the right to kill, since as an anthropological matter this distinction is a relatively recent one; and he ponders whether this and similar insights might "help us distinguish between giving doctors the right to remove life support systems and the right of the terminally ill to demand lethal drugs from the same doctor." Judge Calabresi wonders whether persons who are prohibited from acquiring lethal drugs will kill themselves in more horrific ways that will be ultimately "more dangerous to society and devastating to survivors. But is it really the case that terminally ill patients would take such measures? And which way would it cut, if they did not? These questions," he adds, "hardly begin to approach the human tragedies, and the deeply held beliefs, that the issues we would have to decide would require us to explore."

Judge Calabresi therefore concludes the court should not at this time address the ultimate merits of the case, and should thus leave it open to the state of New York to enact new laws prohibiting assisted suicide. For if the New York legislature does so in a way that explains the legislature's *reasons* for reenacting such prohibitions, then perhaps those reasons will survive the court's constitutional scrutiny:

> I [will for now] take no position on whether such prohibitions, or other more finely drawn ones, might be valid under either or both [the due process or equal protection clauses], were New York to reenact them *while articulating the reasons* for the distinctions it makes in its laws, *and expressing the grounds* for the prohibitions themselves. [emphasis added]

Note the remarkable cognitive dissonance implicit in this conclusion. Judge Calabresi is far too intelligent not to appreciate what he calls the "extreme complexity" of the moral conundrums at the heart of such an excruciating political and ethical issue as that of assisted suicide. And yet so deep is the cultural faith in both reason in general, and in what the American legal system treats as the extraordinary rational powers of judges, that Judge Calabresi still finds himself impelled to assert that the law both requires and (we must suppose) enables he and his judicial brethren to evaluate and resolve the various moral questions posed by these matters in some rational, and indeed rationally superior way.

Perhaps the business of judging the law simply doesn't allow for the cultivation of that quality of sympathetic imagination Keats called "negative capability"—"that is when man is capable of being in uncertainties, Mysteries, doubts, without any irritable reaching after fact & reason." Indeed, we can suppose that as a practical matter the psychological pressures of judging require the *elimination* of real ambivalence. But to lack such ambivalence about the proper resolution of a deep cultural conflict must itself require a kind of blindness: an intellectual blindness that makes one incapable of perceiving, or at least taking seriously, those same uncertainties, mysteries, and doubts of which Keats wrote.

One of the continual puzzles of political, legal, and academic life is how a highly intelligent person, fully capable of appreciating the tremendously complex and indeed fundamentally inexplicable elements involved in undertaking essentially contestable ethical judgments, is somehow transformed into the sort of happy idiot who is certain—beyond a reasonable doubt, as it were—of "the sanctity of unborn life," or of a woman's "constitutional right to choose." Reader, do such persons possess some enzyme that you and I lack? Is some chemical released in their brains that allows them to believe they have "reasoned" to these conclusions? It is a deep and abiding mystery.

Many a time I have sat among superbly educated, intellectually gifted legal academics, listening to a subtle discussion of some deeply controversial issue, waiting for that inevitable moment when the miracle of ethical judgment will be performed. For at that moment this group of talented legal scholars will metamorphose (with the possible exception of this or that perverse nonconformist) into a veritable warren of rationalist rabbits, their heads bobbing in a blissful community of agreement, as the question is begged and the magic words uttered: "justice," "fairness," "principle," and of course, "reason."

Now if this sort of group is sufficiently homogenous, its members may never even notice that their agreement is a product of that homogeneity rather than of any inherent ability to reason to valid ethical conclusions. Richard Posner has described how, when he was a student there, the faculty of the Harvard Law School was almost exclusively white and male, and ran the ideological gamut of American politics from mildly liberal to mildly conservative. Naturally this particular group found that on most issues of public controversy most of its members proved to be reasonable men. Today law faculties display considerably greater gender and ethnic diversity, and even some real ideological divisions. Nevertheless, the vast majority of law professors are liberal-left Democrats who can be counted on to vote, however grudgingly, for Bill Clinton. It seems almost as if the institutions that employ these persons manage to perceive, however dimly, that if this kind of relative ideological blandness isn't maintained, the comforting facade of the powers of legal reason can't be maintained, either.

Consider in this light a review written by the neo-conservative scholar Thomas Sowell critiquing two recent books on affirmative action, one strongly supporting and the other just as strongly condemning the practice. The review is entitled "Affirmative Action: Logic vs. Sentiment"; and, whether or not Professor Sowell is actually responsible for that title, it captures the essence of his review. Here again we find the rationalist illusion rightly criticized by Robin West: the fallacy that this sort of issue is amenable to resolution through the employment of logical argument and the citation of empirical data, rather than through appeals to our sentimental faculties and axiomatic moral beliefs. The review ends with these words: "Still, there is much to be said for reading both books—if only to discover ... that there are issues on which good arguments cannot be found on both sides. Affirmative action is one of those issues."

Of course the irony here is that Sowell's equally dogmatic liberal-left opponents would be in complete agreement with his theoretical observation—although needless to say they would draw precisely the opposite practical conclusion.

What sort of "reasoned discourse" can we suppose is going to take place between people who think this way? Isn't it obvious that in order to maintain the rationalist illusion that this type of issue can be resolved through the employment of reason the representatives of one or another of these camps must be ignored, silenced, ostracized, eliminated, or otherwise precluded from participating in what Professor Nussbaum calls with a certain benign complacency "our human and historical practices of choice and selection?"

For in the end do we—indeed, can we—make such choices by virtue of what reason demands? It appears that those who are prone to think of deep social conflict as a sort of ongoing graduate seminar in moral philosophy believe we can. Yet when the power of the state is employed for the purpose of resolving such conflicts we do not call that force "reason," but rather "law," "politics," or "war," depending on the implicit levels of ideological obfuscation and explicit levels of state violence to which the sovereign power must resort.

Consider one of the most spectacular examples of this process, drawn from the central event of American history. The debate over slavery was not resolved, despite numerous attempts to do so, through either public debate, judicial decision, or legislative enactment. Several million Americans fought and killed their fellow countrymen with ferocious and unrelenting zeal to resolve an issue before which, like all fundamental issues of ethical and political judgment, the power of reason lay impotent.

Today nothing is more "self-evident" than the evil of slavery. In our lazy, ahistorical fashion we more or less assume we have been granted some sort of moral perspicacity regarding this practice that was unavailable to the most of the world's civilizations, and indeed to our own great-grandparents. Yet if we lack the negative capability to suspend our relentlessly judgmental natures—if we cannot exercise the sympathetic powers to place ourselves in the historical context of other, very different times and places—then this truly represents a failure of the capacity for rational judgment. If you and I, that is, cannot imagine ourselves as zealous and wholehearted apologists for the peculiar institution of the American South—if we cannot imagine insisting, with Professor Nussbaum's favorite philosopher, that the proper use of reason demonstrates beyond cavil that some men are born slaves—then we have been burdened (or blessed) not with the gifts of reason, but rather with all-too-human limits on our powers of moral imagination and historical sympathy.

10

THE WAY OF RENUNCIATION

The perfect way is without difficulty,
Save that it avoids picking and choosing.
Only when you stop liking and disliking
Will all be clearly understood.

SENG-TS'AN, *Treatise on Faith in the Mind*

In the cold calculus of the utilitarian the American law school is a classic barrier to entry, designed to maintain a professional cartel. From a democratic viewpoint it is a seminary for the production of a mystifying priestcraft, whose obscurantist incantations help legitimate the power of the social and cultural elite. In academic terms it is a mostly fraudulent operation that teaches neither theory nor practice, but instead functions as the equivalent of a foreign service academy that would show its charges *Goldfinger* several hundred times before sending them forth to conduct trade talks with Austria.

Should it then perhaps be abolished altogether? After all, no other legal system in the world requires three years of postgraduate schooling before a person can undertake the most routine matter of client representation or courtroom advocacy. Indeed, some hint of the latent dissatisfaction with this system is found in such curiosities as the maverick presidential candidate Morry Taylor making a pledge to close down American law schools for ten years one of the major proposals of his quixotic campaign.

It should be unnecessary to add that nothing of the kind is going to happen. Advocating the elimination or even the significant paring back of the American law school (making it an undergraduate program, for example, or a college major followed by some sort of postgraduate apprenticeship) would be a quintessentially rationalist response to an institution that survives, and even thrives, because it fills a deep cultural need for the maintenance of some atavistic set of rituals that will obscure the inescapably troublesome and often tragic relationship between moral belief, political practice, and social power.

What we call "law" must, at moments of great social and moral complexity, deny that complexity and give definitive responses in what are always less than definitive circumstances. For the legal scholar this can be a hard truth. Given the rhetorical requirements of legal argument, and the practical exigencies of legal decision making, it isn't an exaggeration to say that the tasks of preparing persons to undertake zealous legal representation and render legal judgment are to some extent incompatible with maintaining strict standards of intellectual honesty. Such is the fate of those of us who must prepare others to wield social power arbitrarily, and yet who must at the same time legitimate that use of power by claiming legal arguments and the decisions that flow from them are impelled by "the law," or "legal principles," or "reason" itself.

But there is no reason why that fate needs to be replicated in all other areas of social life. Still, in America today, the habits of the legal mind and the structure of legal argument have become so widespread that it often seems that most persons who dominate American public life *are* lawyers, or at least talk and act very much as if they were. And it may well be the case that the consequences—for both the broader culture and for the future American law—of this wholesale juridification of American life are only beginning to be felt.

Natural Born Lawyers

Lawyers are often impelled by their professional obligations to become something akin to emotional prostitutes; that is, to be persons whose public personae require the simulation of inauthentic affective states as a condition of their compensation. In the context of ongoing litigation the most common of these simulated emotions is outrage: a lawyer trying a case must always be ready to express what seems like genuine outrage at the drop of the proverbial hat.

Perhaps because so many politicians are lawyers, or perhaps simply because everyone has seen facets of the lawyerly persona exhibited in so many different contexts of social conflict, various dramaturgical requirements of the adversary system are now being assimilated gradually into all forms of public conversation. In particular, the simulation of outrage has become a seemingly permanent part of the broader political culture. National television programs featuring supposedly sophisticated political commentary, such as "Crossfire," "The McLaughlin Group," and "The Capital Gang," provide examples of how lawyerly rhetoric and its accompanying emotional simulation have become key elements in the dramatic logic of public political discourse. One of these programs even concludes with each commentator choosing an "outrage of the week"— which often enough turns out to be some display of political inauthenticity that merely mirrors the melodrama of the commentator's own stylized performance.

But such displays are hardly limited to jaded sophisticates near the centers of national power. Right here in placid, provincial Boulder, Colorado, there is no issue too small—no dispute about the singing of "Silent Night" in the high school auditorium, or the display of Halloween decorations in the common areas of a housing development—that it will not be accompanied by emotional pyrotechnics from amateur litigators, complete with exhaustive citations to the Boulder City Charter and the U.S. Constitution, if not to the Magna Carta and the Universal Declaration of Human Rights.

Yet unlike real litigators, those who mimic the professional personae of lawyers are usually unaware that lawyers are almost always faking it. So it is that when a Boulder citizens' group expresses "outrage" over a zoning variance that will allow a McDonald's to be built, its various members really *are* outraged. In this way the gradual juridification of public debate leads to a general cheapening of political discourse. Such a generalization of courtroom language and affect to all matters of public controversy causes people to use the same terms to condemn a proposed slowing in the rate of growth of Medicare outlays as they do to lament the practice of genocide in

Bosnia or Rwanda. Eventually the claim that one is outraged is automatically translated into the subtextual language of the law, and hence is understood to mean merely that the speaker disagrees with some other person's view of a matter.

All this mimicry of legal affect and its accompanying language is, in part, a product of the remarkable romanticism that surrounds the cultural ideal of law in American society. The Solomonic judge, the passionate defense attorney, the stout-hearted juror: these are the figures that dominate the American idealization of law: these are the cultural representations of legality that help produce that profound fascination with law so characteristic of both elite and popular American culture. The breathless analysis of all things Simpson on Geraldo Rivera's nightly television show is in its symbolic essence replicated by the equally starry-eyed reportage of the latest joint plurality opinion from the Supreme Court found amid the staid, solemn pages of the *New York Times*. This romantic vision of law overlooks or ignores the fact that American courts are now gigantic bureaucracies, processing more than 30,000,000 lawsuits per year, with all the attendant evils that mark enormous, anonymous government institutions more or less run by a permanent mandarin class of faceless functionaries.

Needless to say this book has not been an argument for anarchy. Too often, debates about the American legal system take place within a context in which doubters are assured both that our system is "the best in the world" (such assurances tend to come from high-status lawyers who know next to nothing about any other legal system), and that the alternative to "the rule of law" is contemporary Bosnia or Lebanon, or some other chaotic corner of the globe. The Federal Rules of Civil Procedure or a Hobbesian war of all against all: such is the "choice" usually presented to us by American rule of law ideology.

But of course the real argument isn't about whether law is a good or a bad thing. Water is without doubt a good thing; indeed some significant amount of the substance is a precondition of life itself. Too much water, however, and we drown.

It is certainly true that in regard to law some contemporary societies resemble the Sahara. This is not America's problem. Indeed, much of our society lies full fathom five beneath the choppy seas of the American legal system; other parts are barely keeping their heads above water; while those that remain safely ensconced on the ever-shrinking mainland eye the advancing tide with a nervous mixture of uncertainty and suspicion.

That suspicion is well warranted by the numerous excesses of American legality: by an obsessive proceduralism that often seems to amount to a belief in process for its own sake; by the system's continual production and increasingly chaotic interpretation of an almost unlimited quantity of massive, procrustean legal documents, monuments to textual hypertrophy that hardly anyone even pretends are coherent or consistently understandable; by its belief that it is possible to both produce comprehensive regulatory regimes, and to predict accurately the effects of essentially ad hoc legal decision making; by its often irrational worship of reason in general and technocratic rationality in particular; and by its accompanying and rationally inexplicable faith in the moral perspicacity of that small group of career bureaucrats called judges.

What will eventually result from such excesses? What, if anything, can be done about them? Among such speculative meanderings my argument concludes.

The Disappearing Railroad Blues

At the turn of the twentieth century the most powerful group of corporations in America was that made up of the great railroad concerns. Having at last linked the vast spaces of the nascent nation together with the completion of the transcontinental rail line, the railroads directly controlled most of the interstate trade across the entire United States, and hence controlled, directly and indirectly, much of the political process that touched on that trade. The fortunes of such men as Cornelius Vanderbilt and Jay Gould were so large that they could by themselves manipulate the movements of entire financial markets; and the estates the railroad barons built as tributes to their social eminence and political power rivaled anything to be found in the ancient principalities of Europe, which indeed they proceeded to plunder for the choicest art that love or money could extract from the old and rotting world.

So omnipotent did these magnates and their companies seem that many a private fortune was passed down through trusts that required the investment of their principal in nothing but railroad stocks. For nothing, surely, could be more certain than the continued dominance of such brilliant entrepreneurs and their all-powerful firms.

Yet within just a generation or two all this was in ruins. By the second half of this century the great American railroads had almost without exception either gone bankrupt, been absorbed by other conglomerates, or been reduced to various conditions of financial ill health. What circumstances led to such a complete fall from grace? Thirty-five years ago, a famous case study in the *Harvard Business Review* gave a compelling account of what happened. The case study demonstrated that the railroads had fallen victim to a classic error of self-understanding, to which especially successful institutions are prone: they had forgotten the true nature of the social need their particular institution was in the business of fulfilling.

The railroad corporations had made the understandable but in the long run fatal mistake of thinking they were in the business of providing *railroads*, when in fact their true economic and social function was to provide *transportation*. In other words, their very success blinded the railroads to the contingent features of that success in the satisfaction of the underlying social needs their enterprise depended on. The railroads had simply defined their social and economic niche at too low a level of abstraction. For even at the moment of these firms' greatest financial, political, and social eminence entrepeneurs such as Henry Ford, the Wright brothers, and others like them were busy with projects that would soon remind everyone that it is always possible to find more than one way to get from here to there cheaply and quickly.

What does the fate of the railroads have to do with the future of the American legal system? After all, in many ways "the rule of law" is to Americans what, for example, cafe au lait, bicycle races, Voltaire, and similar cultural artifacts are to the French: that thing that makes us what we are. America, perhaps uniquely among great nations, has a public culture that relies for much of its identity on the particular structure of the current political regime. Try to imagine the United States, like most ordinary modern nations, choosing to formally adopt a significantly different system of government from what we have at present. It is difficult to do. As parochial as our own peculiar concept of the rule of law may be, we nevertheless know or sense that this concept is in many ways identical with the constitutive ideology of our public political culture.

All of which is to say it is very difficult for Americans to accept that any legal system is at bottom merely a complex network of politically agreed on norms of conduct. "The law" is a grandiloquent term for something that would more accurately be called "social coordination and dispute processing:" how, as it were, to get from here to there on certain parts of the social and cultural map. Indeed, the semantics of the word "law" provide a good example of the ways in which the structure of our language can influence our basic perception of reality. Clumsy as it is, the phrase "social coordination and dispute processing" isn't fraught with the portentous cultural baggage of "law," resonating as that word does with echoes of our deepest theological, tautological, and scientific beliefs (God's law, the laws of mathematics, the law of gravity, and so forth). Perhaps the word *law* itself plays an important role in our tendency to confuse the process of making up a bunch of rules to help us muddle through the conflicts and complexities of social life with the altogether more grandiose projects evoked by that awesome signifier.

A system of social coordination and dispute processing is just that: it isn't an adequate secular substitute for religion, or even for the impure uncertainties of political life. Yet with the contemporary collapse among American cultural elites of both traditionally religious and overtly political forms of metaphysical belief, *our* law tends more and more to become both the patriotism of the deracinated and the de facto faith of the apostate. Hence the tacit ideology of American civic life has become burdened with the widespread delusion that something called "the rule of law" can succeed where politics and culture fail.

In America today what I have called the juridical saturation of reality becomes more and more of a fact of daily life. And not merely in America: in Europe, for example, the particular political and social cultures of more than a dozen nations are being swallowed up by that monument to the pretensions of technocratic rationality, the European Union. All over the so-called developed world, law is manifesting itself as a kind of cultural madness, whereby hyperrational modes of decision making are employed in a vain attempt to resolve rationally what are rationally irresolvable moral and political conflicts.

Yet in this regard as in so many others the United States remains a cultural leader. For instance, to visit California—that contemporary epicenter of everything the world thinks of as American—is to be struck by how this of all places has become a juridically saturated space. Wherever one turns in the public fora of that problematic Eden elaborate legal texts silently blare at the citizenry, giving them "notice" of this, warning of the hazards of that: prohibiting and requiring, admonishing and advising. Indeed in the midst of an idle afternoon I have found myself wondering what it must be like to be a pregnant woman in the land of the acacia, where it seems every public place features some textual reminder of all the potentially damaging things such women are prohibited from doing to those entities they nevertheless retain a constitutionally guaranteed right to "terminate."

For my part, it is true I once anointed my body in the voluptuous surf of Zuma Beach, on a day when the red flags prohibiting swimming blew rigid in the Santa Ana wind. Still, I have been thanked for not smoking by Kenneth, a purveyor of Chilean sea bass served with organically grown vegetables in a Healthmark-approved cream sauce, infused with a hint of cilantro; I have not driven in the commuter lane or presumed O. J. Simpson to be anything but innocent until proven guilty; I haven't imported produce bearing Mediterranean fruit flies, or operated a motor vehicle that failed to meet the most rigorous of current emission standards; and I have, to the best of my knowledge, respected everyone's judicially guaranteed rights to be treated equally in all matters without regard to race, color, creed, ethnic origin, age, gender, sexual orientation, marital or domestic partnership arrangements, physical or mental disability, Vietnam-era veterans status, political beliefs, aesthetic handicaps, or habits of personal hygiene. I have, in short, tried hard to be good.

But it is hard to be good in California. It may be that where the continent runs out manifest destiny becomes especially manifest. Or perhaps it is just the hypertrophied nature of everything in that extreme land. For whatever reason, it is in California that American cultural tendencies tend to bloom in their most virulent form. Here in California one gets the clearest glimpse of how America, the beautiful, unique country, is being slowly strangled by its own obsessive will toward legal perfectionism; toward getting it "right"; toward "solving" through juridical intervention all moral, political, and cultural problems, no matter how insoluble those problems may actually be.

The hypertrophied rationalism of American law is a product of trying too hard to be good: of failing to accept that law is always a somewhat crude and potentially destructive social steering mechanism, that works best when it remains a tacit presence in the social background. Instead we Americans insist on subjecting ourselves to a dictatorship of the bureaucratic: one in which the answer to every important social conflict inevitably involves more rules and procedures, more rights and obligations, more "reasons" and "principled justifications" given in the course of constructing ever-more complex analytic and rhetorical circles for choosing to do this rather than that—in brief, more law.

I write these sentences on the first day of the Oklahoma City bombing trial: a trial that seems certain to last for several months (of course any appellate process arising out of it is likely to take many years.)* Is there any good reason to believe the vast social resources

---

*Timothy McVeigh's trial lasted three months. In all that time, his lawyers managed to produce essentially no exculpatory evidence that might have even begun to counterbalance the government's overwhelmingly redundant demonstration of their client's guilt; they did, however, bill the American public approximately $10,000,000 for their services. It says something about what we have come to expect of our law that the McVeigh trial has been hailed as a paragon of expeditiousness and efficiency.

being devoted to this and similar juridical inquisitions produce better (more just, more accurate) results than would a well-designed set of more modest proceedings each lasting, say, a week? Exactly what benefits are the American people supposed to be receiving when they so graciously foot the very considerable bill resulting from our legal system's obsessive devotion to what it calls "the rule of law"?

In its pursuit of such underinvestigated questions this book has suggested that much of the baroque complexity of modern American law represents what is at best a wasteful multiplication of transaction costs, and at worst a symptom of a species of institutionalized mental illness. There can be little doubt that, for most of our legal establishment, this idea is almost literally unthinkable. After all, a critique cannot even begin to be heard without some minimal willingness to consider the possible truth of its claims. And, given the current cultural dominance of American rule of law ideology, the idea that much of the basic structure of American law might be a pointless or even pathological outgrowth of various rationalist delusions is likely to be dismissed out of hand as nothing less than bizarre. The sacrosanct status of law in American culture may well ensure that, for the orthodox legal mind, a sincere engagement with any fundamental criticism of the legal system is simply not an option.

Indeed, the American legal establishment often seems to treat "going to law" almost as if this were a good thing *in and of itself*. From this perspective, the extensive employment of the legal process is not merely necessary, but actually desirable. Now we should note that to criticize the implicit foundational axiom of American legal ideology, that is, "more law = good/less law = bad," is not to criticize law *per se*. No one, for example, is likely to take the observation that armies and hospitals are in a sense necessary evils as a criticism of the medical or military arts. Still, imagine a culture in which doctors thought chemotherapy was so wonderful they encouraged people to undergo treatment whether they were sick or not, or in which generals routinely sang paeans to trench warfare and saturation bombing. Yet more than one prominent American legal academic has questioned the desirability of out-of-court settlements, on the ground that such settlements deprive the legal system of opportunities to make more law! (Such suggestions provide yet more evidence of how the American legal elite has much the same orientation toward law that McDonald's has toward hamburgers—and for many of the same reasons.)

Another central theme of this book has been that the excesses of American rule of law ideology are in large part enabled by our unwillingness to accept that reason, when properly employed, works to make its further employment superfluous. Reason, that is, works ironically toward its own effacement. When it works well, it takes the reasoner to a point in the decision process where the use of reason no longer helps. In this regard law is, as we have seen, paradigmatic. Hence "legal reasoning" works well precisely to the extent that we are not conscious of its presence. Outside a legal equilibrium zone law tends to be both an invisible and a powerful factor in the maintenance of social cohesion. By contrast within such a zone the inevitable contradictions in the legal rules such situations produce are clearly visible, and as a consequence the rules themselves are rendered relatively useless. Faced with such legal and social contradictions, we cannot decide efficiently processed legal disputes on the basis of "reason." We merely decide.

The essential fallacy of legal rationalism is thus to think that what works well in moderation will work even better in large doses. So deep is this belief that when the more extreme manifestations of legal reason fail altogether we tend to manifest a willful blindness to this failure, or we undertake what soon become perverse efforts to perfect systems of rules that, by the nature of the problems they address, can't be perfected. When neither of these strategies work we do what courts often do and simply indulge in magical thinking, assuming, for example, that because a court ends its opinion with the phrase "it is so ordered," "it" is both going to happen, and to produce a series of predictable social effects.

Just as this book has not been an argument for any particular political or social theory, it has also not argued against "reason," whatever that word might be thought to mean. Rather, it has tried to remind readers of both the limitations of all modes of rational inquiry, and of how at some point the pursuit of reasoned judgment becomes not merely inefficient, but actually irrational. Consider one last example: we might compare the diminishing marginal utility of what is called "legal reasoning" to the time and labor invested in cleaning a house when guests are going to visit. Suppose that in forty-five minutes the house can be made quite presentable; while three hours are required to achieve something Martha Stewart would applaud. Now arguments about whether we should spend one or two or three hours cleaning the house can be assimilated to a rational choice model of human decision making; that is, we can argue in such a context about whether it makes sense to spend twice as much time on the project to get the house 10 percent cleaner. By contrast, a decision to spend forty hours cleaning the house cannot be analyzed usefully from within a framework that assumes rational choice. Indeed, such behavior is evidence of something else altogether: of a will to a kind of obsessive-compulsive excess, whose excessive character is not only inefficient, but will actually end up doing damage to the objects of its attention.

This book *has* argued that, in sufficiently complex decisional situations, rational analysis calls for arational decision making. This fairly elementary insight flies in the face of the American belief in cadres of "experts," specially gifted persons who will supply answers unavailable to the rest of us. We buy more books than the rest of the world combined telling us how to flatten our stomachs and improve our careers; advising us how to make love, and in what ways we should raise our children; books whose glib authors assure us *they* can tell us how to deal with *our* childhood tragedies and adult addictions, and who promise us psychological self-actualization, personal happiness, and spiritual enlightenment in seven easy steps. Naturally we then turn to law as a source of political and moral expertise, and just as naturally become infuriated with lawyers when they reveal themselves as having no more insight into such matters than anyone else. Nevertheless much like Charlie Brown, running once again to kick the football that, every autumn, Lucy yanks away at the last possible moment, we keep coming back for more—ignoring the evident absurdity of expecting courts to give compelling or even adequate reasons for accepting or rejecting this or that answer to some fundamental moral question on which we ourselves cannot agree.

Because of such rationalist excesses the American legal system is in some danger of being treated as roughly by the coming decades as the great American railroads were treated by the century that has almost passed. American law, that is, may well find itself betrayed by its own overweening pride in having succeeded in its quest to bring so much of American life under its sway. As a consequence of the legal system's increasing tendency to deny the true nature of its crucial but relatively modest role as a social coordination and dispute processing mechanism, our law is becoming so elaborate, so hypertrophied, so pointlessly complex, and hence so unnecessarily expensive that alternate modes of getting from here to there on the social map are already springing up all around us. Accountants are taking over the tax business; insurance companies are eliminating real estate title searches; private firms are setting up their own modes of dispute processing; mediation and arbitration services of every kind are booming. And of course various militant ideologies of the far right serve as disconcerting reminders of how considerably more radical forms of dissent against what is called the rule of law are already simmering.

Such nascent rebellions against law's empire are thus to some extent products of law's own success. The current cultural dominance of legal modes of thought—the belief that political and ethical decisions are legitimate only to the extent they can be crammed into the conceptual categories of legal reasoning—helps reinforce a legal culture in which other modes of decision making are treated as degraded versions of law, rather than as potentially valuable alternatives to law's imperialistic grasp. Indeed, partially because of the desire to control the cultural power it wields, the category of law itself has in recent decades often been reduced even further to encompass no more than the legal process ideology of one particular generation of judges, lawyers, and law professors. It is as if the entire category of transportation came to mean only "automobiles," which in turn was usually understood to mean only Buick Skylarks.

Under such cultural conditions we could anticipate that Buick Skylarks would get extraordinarily expensive. That, in the short run, would be good for General Motors but bad for America. But in the long run, the onerous price of these particular cars would itself begin to corrode the ideological underpinnings of the narrow conception of transportation, and consequently people would start looking for other ways to travel. The initial reaction to this development on the part of those who had profited from the narrow conception would be to claim that driving nothing but Buick Skylarks was integral to our national concept of transportation. It would be said that the notion of driving a Ford or a Chrysler was contrary to fundamental American values (as for traveling by bicycle the very idea would be dismissed out of hand, given that it involved a blatant contradiction in terms). Such delegitimation strategies might work for a time, but eventually either the price of Skylarks would have to come down, or Buick would find itself teetering on the brink of extinction.

Will what is now called the rule of law go the way of the rule of the railroads? Today, surrounded as we are by an anarchic panopticon of rules, and moving as we do through an ever-more juridically saturated social space, the very question may seem absurd. Yet when we remember what Joseph Schumpeter called those "gusts of creative destruction" by which advanced capitalism reshapes the world, and when we add to this the (closely related) theme of regenerative pragmatism that has characterized much of American history, we should also recall that this century has already witnessed the destruction of many proud and apparently immutable institutions and ideologies whose demise has left behind little trace of what once seemed their unassailable social power. Great locomotives that once annihilated the endless miles of wheat fields shimmering across our northern plains, their whistles piercing the dark veil of humid summer nights with a heartrending shriek, are today remembered only by rusted-out tracks hidden amid the tall prairie grass: iron rails on a long road to nowhere.

The Way of Renunciation

What then is to be done? Given the argument of this book any answer to that question risks falling under the spell of the same rationalist illusions the argument has described. Law is in its own way as habit-forming as cocaine, and thus I—a lawyer—can hardly claim immunity from the temptation to outline grand reforms and definitive solutions, to recommend five-part tests and twelve-step plans: "Hello my name is ____, and I'm a jurismaniac."

What is the solution to breaking our addiction to solutions? This is our paradox. Perhaps we can find the answer by renouncing the search for answers.

The hypertrophied rationalism of American law is a product of trying to undertake formal analysis in a legal system within which any real commitment to formalism has broken down; of attempting to reach accurate empirical conclusions without anything like the necessary data; and of engaging in covert moral theorizing without a moral theory. Of course the rationalist response to intimations that any of this might be the case is to toss oil on the fire: we must construct a better justification for honoring formal rules; we must invent new methodologies for gathering the necessary facts; we are morally obliged to discover an adequate moral theory. Might there be a better way?

The Federal Land Policy and Management Act, Pub. L. 94-579, 90 Stat. 2743, codified at 43 U.S.C. sections 1701–1784 (1982), provided that holders of various mining claims to federal land were required "prior to December 31" of every year to file certain documents with the relevant government agencies or lose their claims. Predictably, a number of claim holders filed their claims on December 31 itself. The federal government denied the validity of the claims on the ground the claim holders had missed the statutory deadline; the claim holders then sued the government.

What will a rationalist analysis of this straightforward conflict entail? (And note again how this case, like most of the cases we have glanced at, is in most respects a remarkably uncomplicated legal dispute. If reason fails to provide convincing answers in this sort of circumstance, how will it fare when faced with more complex formal and empirical ambiguities?) We can anticipate that a legal actor who wants the government to win will try to show the law requires the "plain meaning" of the statutory deadline to be enforced. This conclusion will then be supported by more or less sophisticated formalist arguments to the effect that the statute's language simply means what it appears to mean, by empirical assertions that this result is what the legislature intended, and by instrumental claims that any other outcome would have various bad consequences for the predictability of legal rules, for federal land management policies, and so on. A legal actor who wants the plaintiffs to win will support that position by making more or less sophisticated anti-formalist arguments about understanding the statute's meaning in the proper interpretive context, by empirical assertions that this result is what the legislature intended, and by instrumental claims that any other outcome would have bad consequences for the rationality of legal rules, for the protection of citizens' fundamental property rights against government encroachment, and so forth.

Notice that despite the straightforward nature of this dispute, these respective rationalist analyses will turn out to be quite expensive. They will necessitate sifting through heaps of legislative history and labyrinths of administrative regulations; and they will require the lawyers and judges involved in the case to spend considerable time constructing, deploying, and evaluating those more or less sophisticated formal, empirical, and moral arguments.

To what end? Will the resolution of this dispute produce a formal rule of legal interpretation that will itself determine or at least usefully predict the outcome of similar interpretive disputes? Will the process of resolution produce convincing evidence of what some significant portion of the 535 members of the U.S. Congress thought about this matter, thus allowing us to do the positive will of the legislature? Will that resolution result in both sufficiently predictable and adequately justified instrumental or ethical consequences?

The dispute resolution process isn't going to accomplish any of these things. Attempts to limit the interpretation of legal meaning to some formal or intentionalist construct can never succeed, if only because over a range of disputes there will always be compelling reasons to follow a variety of interpretive approaches. The search for legislative intent itself will usually involve some question of such conceptual complexity or bureaucratic obscurity that the interpreter

will at best be able to discover that few or no members of the legislature ever considered any such question. Attempts to produce
definitive instrumental or deontological reasons for deciding a difficult case in a particular fashion are equally hopeless, both because of
the practical impossibility of making accurate predictions about the
likely instrumental outcomes of particular legal decisions, and
because of the theoretical impossibility of producing, within an ethically pluralist culture such as our own, compelling moral justifications for politically controversial results.

But surely, the rationalist ideologue asserts, we must decide legal
disputes on the basis of good reasons. Why? Because rationalist
dogma declares such a rationally justified decision necessary and we,
indulging in a fairly spectacular non sequitur, assume such a decision
is therefore possible? This mania for *giving reasons* is the very
essence of jurismaniacal excess, and indeed is the source of our culture's irrational addiction to "reason" in general.

There is a wonderful sketch by the Monty Python comedy troupe
called "The Royal Society for Putting Things on Top of Other
Things." The Royal Society for Putting Things on Top of Other
Things meets annually to evaluate the performance of the group's
membership in the carrying out of the Society's mission over the
course of the previous year. At the beginning of the sketch the
President of the Society calls the meeting to order and notes that he
himself, on his way to this very meeting, noticed several things not
on top of other things. This announcement is met by cries of
"Shame, shame!" which the President calms by pointing out that "if
there were not one thing that was not on top of some other thing,
we would be nothing but a meaningless group of men who gathered
together for no good purpose." Then follow the reports of several
chapters ("our Australasian chapter, and various groups affiliated
with the Australasian chapter, have in the last year placed no less
than twenty-two things on top of other things") that continue until
the representative of the Staffordshire chapter causes a sensation by
admitting that his group has failed to place a single thing on top of
some other thing. When asked by the President to explain this
extraordinary behavior, the representative replies meekly, "Well sir,

it's just that most of the members in Staffordshire feel the whole thing's a bit silly," to which the outraged President responds, "*Silly?* What do you mean, silly? Hm . . . I suppose it is, a bit. What have we been doing wasting our lives with all this nonsense?" (General cries of "Hear, hear.") "Right then. Meeting adjourned forever."

It should be obvious the Legal Society for Giving Rationally Compelling Reasons isn't going to be adjourning any time soon. The most we can hope for is that some way might be found to make its meetings a little shorter, and the catering bill a little less. Here then is my own tentative contribution toward that more modest goal.

Law is suffering.

Suffering arises from the desire to get it right.

Rid yourself of that desire and rid yourself of suffering.

To eliminate the desire meditate on these other truths.

We might call this "the way of renunciation." For in law, the desire to find the right answer is always inflamed precisely by our failure to do any such thing. When the holders of mining claims on federal lands file their claims for 1996 on September 21, 1996, or January 18, 1997, we feel no desire to find the right legal answer to the question of whether their claims are valid because that answer is already clear. It is when the law *cannot* give us an answer that we will demand it do so. The attempt to gratify this desire produces both the excesses of modern regulatory schemes and the neurotic structure of appellate court decision making. Like the fabled donkey imagined by the medieval scholastics, who starves to death because he is exactly equidistant from two stacks of hay and therefore can't decide rationally to which stack he should go, we demand dispositive reasons for choosing where there are none. Less principled than Buridan's ass, we then "discover"—at great fiscal and psychological expense—some answer that must be arrived at more or less arbitrarily, while still insisting that this particular outcome was impelled by the law, or legal principles, or reason itself.

How then would this way of renunciation deal with the conflict of the mining claims? Should the apparent plain meaning of the statutory deadline be enforced? Answering *this* question rationally would require comparing the virtue of enforcing formal certainty (but only *formal* certainty, as we can predict that a deadline that excludes only the last day of the year will be misread to include it) against the desirability of enforcing the deadline the legislature would have chosen if its members had in fact considered this precise question. It would also require considering whether the expectation interest of claim holders was a more compelling ethical consideration than the potential negative effects on federal lands that might arise from continuing to honor those expectations, as well as evaluating what those effects were likely to be. A truly comprehensive rational analysis would also attempt to take into consideration the possible consequences for future decision making of either appearing to follow, or revising through "interpretation," apparently clear but rationally inexplicable legal rules.

On the other hand by recognizing the rational intractability of such questions a legal decision maker would acknowledge the dispute's presence in an analytic equilibrium zone, and would realize that the question of the dispute's proper resolution was not usefully amenable to more extensive rational analysis. The court's analysis of the facts and its subsequent holding in the case might then read something like this: "Judgment for the plaintiff." Or if it is simply a cultural imperative for legal decision makers to give reasons for their decisions the opinion might read, "Because of the plain meaning of the statute's text, the claims fail." Or, if you prefer, "Because the legislature did not intend to bar claims filed on the last day of the year, the claims are valid." It is just possible that, if appellate opinions looked even a little more like this, lawyers would be less prone to waste social resources researching and writing eighty-page briefs that attempt to address every possible permutation of a legal argument, or sifting through the textual arcana of legislatures and agencies—much of which is itself a reaction to the excesses of legal reasoning—in a vain search for whatever scrap of evidence they hope will tip what they imagine to be the exquisitely balanced scales of juridical judgment.

As difficult as it is for most contemporary legal thinkers to imagine a dispute about mining claims being disposed of in this fashion, it is quite impossible for them to conceive of issues such as abortion or euthanasia being dealt with along similar lines. What legitimacy would courts have if they decided such excruciatingly difficult moral and political questions through undisguised acts of fiat? Yet this objection overlooks two points. First, as a practical matter, it is possible that in the long run poorly disguised acts of fiat are even more corrosive of perceived judicial legitimacy (they are certainly more expensive). More fundamentally, if such momentous questions must in the end be answered by arational fiat, it is to say the least unclear why we would want courts to monopolize the business of supplying those answers. Of course the rationalist demands not fiat, but reason. Fine—I demand nonfattening hot fudge, the love of Uma Thurman, and the starting second-base job for the Detroit Tigers. We'll see who waits longer.

To paraphrase Samuel Johnson, a man becomes a judge to forget the pain of being a man. We each of us want to believe that the act of passing judgment—of declaring we "know" affirmative action is wrong or that abortion is a constitutional right—somehow removes us from behind those veils of ignorance philosophers and kings have struggled so impotently to rend. And yet to believe the rationalist illusions undergirding this particular belief can be swept aside through the persuasive force of reasoned argument is itself but another rationalist illusion.

Still, law and legal reason are also the simulacra of real community. The way of renunciation is just one example of how, here and there, it remains possible to acknowledge both the strengths and limitations of the law and its reasons. For all the hubris of law's empire—for all the vanity of its claims to know what cannot be known of the quality of mercy, of justice and injustice, good and evil —the invisible law of our ordinary lives still plays a modest but crucial role in the maintenance of both our political communities and our social selves. To renounce the imperial claims of legal reason we need merely remember what so much of our culture conspires to make us forget: that in all truth we have neither seen the tree of knowledge, nor yet tasted of its strange and bitter fruit.

Index